GERALD HOBERMAN

THE ART OF COINS
AND THEIR PHOTOGRAPHY

AN ILLUSTRATED PHOTOGRAPHIC TREATISE
WITH AN INTRODUCTION TO NUMISMATICS

By Gerald Hoberman

Fellow of the Royal Numismatic Society, London.

SPINK & SON LIMITED
FOUNDED 1666
in association with
LUND HUMPHRIES PUBLISHERS LIMITED
LONDON

THE ART OF COINS
AND THEIR PHOTOGRAPHY

FOR HAZEL, RICHARD, JOANNE AND MARC

Photography, concept & production co-ordination by the Author

Editor: Nicola Helen Legg

Design: Gerhard Schwekendiek of Janice Ashby Design Studios

Line illustrations: Tobie Beele

Index: Ethleen Lastovica

Lithography & typesetting: Hirt & Carter (Pty) Limited

Printed & bound by: ABC Press (Pty) Limited

First edition 1981.
Published by Spink & Son, London, 5, 6 & 7 King Street, St James's, London SW1
in association with Lund Humphries Publishers, 26 Lichfield Street, London WC2.
Distributed to the book trade by Lund Humphries Publishers.
Printed in the Republic of South Africa.

Contents

Circa 1509 - 1567
TWO TAX GATHERERS
By MARINUS van
Reymerswaele

These grotesque gentlemen appear to be municipal tax collectors for the Dutch town of Reymerswaele in Zeeland. The principal character on the left is compiling an account of taxes on wine, beer, fish, etc. Several of the gold coins in the lower righthand corner have been identified as Écus d'or au soleil of François Ier and two of the large silver coins as Joachimstalers of Schlick which have assisted in the dating of this painting. The timeless lure of money and the omnipresent and relentless tenacity of the tax collector are masterfully portrayed with a brand of satire usually meted out to mothers-in-law.

Preface

Gerald Hoberman, an enthusiastic numismatist and photographer by profession, has for some time explored the possibilities inherent in coin photography.

His main object in writing this book was to accentuate the artistry and the skill involved in both the coins themselves and their photographic reproduction.

The photographic section highlights this objective: the coins are shown both in actual size and enlarged, and the standard of photography is quite outstanding. Gerald Hoberman has succeeded in bringing to coin photography a degree of perfection rarely, if ever, previously achieved.

The author has selected a group of coins based mainly on the merit of their design, including a wide range of types and denominations. In describing the coins, he has provided detailed descriptions (including heraldic terminology) enabling the collector to enjoy every possible feature of the design.

Altogether this is a most unusual book – put together with the utmost attention to detail. It will appeal equally to the numismatist as well as to the student of photography or art, and the former will perhaps discover a great deal more to the design of coins than previously realised.

Douglas Liddell

Introduction

The object of this book is to try to convey the enjoyment and wonder that I have derived from numismatics. As for many of us, coin collecting began during early childhood with the acquisition of small change given to me by relatives returning from holidays abroad. My interest was later stimulated during time spent in London some years ago as a professional photographer. I was fortunate to be commissioned to photograph priceless rarities entrusted to me by an old gentleman and was deeply moved by the ability of the ancient die engravers to transport the spirit of the ancient world through two and a half millennia by their masterful techniques and sense of style. During this assignment I felt a compelling need to do full justice to the task, from a sense of deep respect for the moneyers of old and a desire to share my appreciation of these works of art with others.

Few people have had the opportunity of gaining access to numismatic rarities to study their artistic merit in detail, owing to the susceptibility of coins to damage and the strict security that must necessarily be imposed. All the coins included in the book have been enlarged and are shown at life size to accentuate the extraordinary skill and artistry of these miniscule masterpieces. A description of each coin is given together with a snippet of information which it is hoped will whet the appetite of the reader, for it is through the in-depth study of a coin's many facets that maximum enjoyment is derived. During the extensive research necessary for this book it became apparent that a great number of collectors, although knowledgeable and eminent numismatists, were unfamiliar with some of the minute detail on coins laid bare through photographic enlargement, and without exception they responded with enthusiasm to the information gleaned or the questions posed. It is hoped that these enlargements together with the text, though possibly at times stating the obvious, will serve to present the coins in a new perspective.

The calligraphy on coins is often a delight and shows the diverse styles of writing and its development. The style of lettering was probably influenced by ligatures and mutations introduced by scribes and the instruments, tools, techniques and materials they used. The individual characters of the coins' legends were drawn, cut and stamped on metal, giving them an appearance quite distinctive from that of the hand written model. They often reflect a national style and their charm is enhanced by the uneven striking or irregular placement of the letters.

Although there are countless publications on numismatics and photography, I was unable to find any books specialising in coin photography with its exacting requirements and its many varied and special problems. Because of the profound influence of photography on numismatics I was prompted to give an insight into the fascinating complexities of coin photography and to record its significance and techniques.

The dramatic effect of photography, a major instrument in the study of numismatics, has widened the scope of its interest, affording millions of people throughout the world access to a vast quantity of numismatic material through photographic reproduction. This is a boon to scholars, and has largely contributed to a rapid escalation in coin collecting and international participation in important sales. With coin photographs both dealers and collectors are able to compare die varieties, to assess the condition and rarity of coins, and thereby to monitor prices. Photography is especially valuable to international coin dealers as a means of offering coins to one or several prospective purchasers simultaneously, while retaining the valuable specimens. This also obviates the need for costly insurance, postage and customs duties. The convenience of instant film is especially useful in this application. Through a wealth of photographically illustrated catalogues, art, and historical works of reference, slides and other visual aids, the student is greatly assisted in gaining a wider perspective and appreciation of the many facets of numismatics. The production of a collection catalogue with photographic illustrations serves as a permanent record providing a readily accessible reference, enhancing the prestige of the collection and improving the prices achieved at auctions. Photography is a most effective aid to lecturers, numismatic societies, and conventions: "One picture is worth ten thousand words". Extensive use is made of photography to publicise new issues of coins and medals by both private and government mints. Photographs and illuminated transparencies can be used very effectively as a point of sale medium; as decorations in banking halls, numismatic conventions and window displays. Photography is invaluable to museums as a means of supporting and/or substituting a numismatic display, or as a means of fitting into sequence rarities outside the museum's collection. Collectors may obtain photographs of coin types they wish eventually to possess, or rare specimens not available, or beyond their financial reach. In pre-planning a collector's *Want List* photographs are most useful, especially in cases where there are numerous varieties of a type varying in artistic merit.

Transparent photographic overlays assist in comparative study of minting techniques by highlighting die positions, cracks and minor variations. Specialised photographic techniques are effective scientific tools in the study of numismatics. Photographic records of archaeological sites where coin hordes have been found are helpful in showing the exact location and other relevant details prior to the hordes being removed and the clusters of coins separated. It is useful to record ancient coins photographically prior to specialised cleaning. Photography is of value to the modern die engraver in the production of dies and in the presentation of designs of both coins and medals for final selection. The photographic medium is often used to authenticate coins by numismatic bodies who issue certificates with photographs and a registered number as a service to members. Photographic comparison is a useful yardstick to coin grading through publications on this frequently controversial subject. A photographic record is invaluable in the *Finger Printing* of coins for positive identification. In the unfortunate event of a theft, robbery or counterfeit this would support evidence in a court of law, and would serve as protection to both the insurer and the insured. Photography affords collectors and investors in coins the facility of appreciating and studying their collection whilst housing their originals in the safety of a bank vault. Through the International Bureau for the Suppression of Counterfeit Coins with its headquarters in London, bulletins are circulated to its members who are collectors, dealers, numismatic department of banks, etc., giving detailed reports with photographic enlargements indicating and identifying counterfeits in circulation, and by so doing, significantly curtailing the activities of forgers internationally.

Such is the significance of photography to numismatics. Its uses and scope will no doubt be further widened by the advances of technology in the future.

From the time the primeval fires of mankind were kindled, man used a system of barter. With the development of civilisation, a medium of exchange was sought, whether the economy was a market economy or based on redistribution by a central authority. Direct barter was often inconvenient, particularly when goods or services were neither needed nor desired by one of the parties. A standard value, as a medium of exchange and convenient store of wealth, was developed using a negotiable instrument desired by all. This varied from one primitive culture to another and consisted of such objects as stone age tools, implements, animal skins, iron, cattle, cowrie shells and salt. With the need of organised societies to trade, these objects often failed to suffice – for example, cattle could not easily be transported great distances without abundant water and grazing, and would be susceptible to weight and stock loss on long journeys. Moreover, animals were not conveniently divisible for making minor payments, and barter was unsuitable for financing armies and levying taxes. Metal as a currency, evolved in the form of ingots, rings, spits and various cast shapes, but these objects were not ideal. They were later made more practical by applying specific standards of weight and purity to them.

The interaction of human agency, cultural fusion and prosperity has throughout the ages been instrumental in the creation of great civilisations. In the ancient world the degree of sophistication in these societies was remarkable. It was probably the increasingly complex activities of Lydia in Asia Minor (Turkey), with Greek Ionia and her other trading partners, that precipitated the introduction of coinage around 650 BC, when it is believed the first coins were struck. Through the democratization of money via personal incentive to the industrious, individual freedom from rigid domination was made possible. The need arose for a medium of exchange that was easily portable, of intrinsically valuable

The Origins of Coinage

Barter system

Negotiable instrument of exchange

Metal currency

First known coins struck

17

metal, with fixed weight and fineness, bearing the inscription and/or device of responsible authority stamped on it. This new economic weapon was to have profound effect on history. Through coinage, trade was often conducted on a large scale over vast distances. Herodotus, the Greek historian, recorded about 430 BC, "So far as we have any knowledge they (the Lydians) were the first nation to introduce the use of gold and silver coins." However, the earliest coins known were not made of gold or silver but of electrum, a pale natural alloy of both these metals, believed to be a separate metal. Electrum, washed downstream from Mount Tmolus, was found in the silt deposits of the Pactolus and Hermus river beds at Sardis, Lydia's capital. Electrum was also mined from the inland Tmolus mountain range and at Mount Sipylus near the coast. Herodotus may have been referring to the later coinage of the Lydian King Croesus (560 – 546 BC). He noted that the white gold (electrum bricks dedicated by the Lydians at Delphi) of similar dimensions to the yellow gold, weighed less. This observation was correct, electrum being less dense than gold. The archaeological excavation at the temple of Artemis, at Ephesus in 1904 – 1905, led by Hogarth, and more recently reappraised by Robinson, dates the earliest coins to the latter half of the seventh century BC. The early coins found at Ephesus were significant as Jacobsthal's meticulous study of objects, discovered at the various archaeological levels on this site, pinpointed the date of their minting to around 600 BC.

By the reign of its last and legendary King Croesus, Lydia encompassed and held stable dominion over the whole plateau of Asia Minor, as far as the river Halys. The incalculably wealthy King Croesus was defeated in battle against Persia at Pteria in 546 BC. After this defeat Lydia became the main satrapy in the west, with Sardis at its centre and close political contact was maintained with the Greek states.

Profound effect of coinage on history

Electrum gold and silver coins

Significant find at Ephesus

Legendary King Croesus

Geographical position of Lydia

AN ACCOUNT OF THE TRANSITION FROM BARTER TO THE USE OF COIN

ARISTOTLE

384 – 322 BC

When the inhabitants of one country
became more dependent on those of another,
and they imported what they needed, and
exported the surplus, money necessarily came
into use. The various necessaries of life are
not easily carried about, and hence men
agreed to employ in their dealings with each
other something which was intrinsically
useful and easily applicable to the purposes of
life; for example, iron, silver and the like.
Of this the value was at first measured by size
and weight, but in process of time they put
a stamp upon it to save the trouble of
weighing and to mark the value.

POLITICS, I. iii.

Techniques of Striking Coin

Natural extension of crafts

Refining techniques

Silver principally used throughout Greece

Practical small change

Predetermined weight and fineness

First known coinage struck

The techniques of the Lydians and the Greeks, in the early production of coin, was a natural extension of the skills practised by the gem and seal engravers, jewellers and masters in the arts of former times. Although their techniques of refining are obscure, they certainly had the practical ability to refine and alloy metals, as is evident from their work passed down to us. In ancient Egypt, according to an account of Agatharchides[*], they refined gold by placing it in an earthenware pot together with lead, tin, salt and barley bran and kept it in a state of great heat for five days. They were less successful in the separation of gold from silver; these two precious metals usually found together were not easily separable. However, the precious metals were easily separated from the baser alloys. Silver was principally used in the production of coin throughout the early Greek world. Gold coin was usually struck during times of crisis and emergency only. Gold though minted in quantity in Persia at that time only later come into general use throughout Greece. The problems of making minor purchases and the need for practical-sized small change brought about the introduction of bronze coin, produced by alloying copper with tin. Bronze coin was in general use from about the fourth century BC. Metal of predetermined fineness was cut from the end of a cylindrical shaped ingot when heated, or cast into moulds of suitable size. The blanks produced were meticulously adjusted to a precise weight, as it is on these principal factors of weight and fineness that the coin's value depends. Certain exceptions exist where copper pieces of the Seleucids and Ptolemies seem to have been cut from plate rather than cast; Indian coins in very early times were also cut as blanks in square form.

The first known coinage was stamped with a punch in various patterns, incuse (intaglio) into the obverse. The reverse was for a brief initial period striated to prevent the blank from shifting on the anvil when struck. The resultant coin was identifiable to its maker, obviating the need to re-weigh it in the event of its passing back to him in the small separate communities in

[*] In Photius, Bibliotheca

20

which these coins circulated. These markings grew in complexity, culminating in increasingly sophisticated coin types, often of great beauty. The device used for striking these types on to a flan is known as a coin die. Dies were made of tempered bronze and *Dies introduced* tin, brass or iron. A design was mapped out on the polished uncut surface of the die and then deeply engraved in intaglio (incuse), to produce the design in high relief when struck. The master die cutter, working with a graver, burin, punch and other tools of his trade, was able to achieve incredible detail and a high degree of artistry. Although no evidence of optical aids exists, they were possibly used in creating the minute detail. The dies were used in various devices such as a fixed anvil with sunken die housing for the obverse die (pile). The flan (prepared coin blank) was heated in a charcoal-fired clay furnace to make it malleable, and placed on the obverse die with tongs. The reverse die (trussell) was positioned and held in place; resounding blows from a heavy hammer struck the obverse and reverse impressions simultaneously on the flan. The coin was then placed in water to temper it. These dies were often capable of producing thousands of coins without obvious signs of wear. The reverse die, being uppermost, literally took more of a hammering and had to be replaced more frequently than the obverse die, which in many cases was well protected, embedded in the anvil. The substitution of worn dies is of great assistance to numismatists in establishing the chronological order of coins, as dates did not appear on early coinage. Later hubbing was introduced whereby the master die was engraved in relief, from which several incuse dies were

PUNCH

REVERSE DIE (trussell)

TONGS

COIN BLANK

OBVERSE DIE (pile)

ANVIL

THE ORIGINS OF COINAGE
SHOWING WHERE
THE EARLY COINS ILLUSTRATED FROM
CIRCA 650~42 BC WERE STRUCK

BLACK SEA

CONSTANTINOPLE
BYZANTIUM

MARA
SEA
S
CYZICUS
ANATOLIA
(TURKEY)
PTERIA
RIVER HALYS
RIVER HALYS
PERSIA
(IRAN)
PYLUS RIVER
HERMUS
SARDIS
PACTOLUS RIVER
PHRYGIA
RIVER TIGRIS
S
SUS
LYDIA
MAGNESIA
PISIDIA
SELGE
MESOPOTAMIA
(IRAQ)
ANTIOCH
HODES
CYPRUS
(LEBANON)
RIVER EUPHRATES
SYRIA
BYBLOS
PHOENICIA
SIDON
SEA
TYRE
BABYLON
PALESTINE
(ISRAEL)
UR
JERUSALEM
ARABIA
KANDRIA
EGYPT
RIVER NILE

23

produced for later or simultaneous use while preserving the original master die. Coin dies were often laid up in racks for a period of time between striking and in many cases rusted, as is evident from the pitting effect on certain coins.

Rusty dies

Occasionally, coins of other cities were overstruck to save the moneyers the task of preparing new blanks. Sometimes victors overstruck their symbols on existing coins as propaganda – a practise that has proved valuable in historical dating.

Overstriking

Many coins exist which are unevenly struck, struck off centre, with unrounded planchets, die cracks, double struck, impact cracks, etc. Perfectly struck hammered coins of antiquity are rare, valuable, and often of great beauty – masterpieces of the die engraver's art.

Minting problems associated with hammered coinage

Coin initially was traded at parity with bullion. However, many mints through the ages gained notoriety by deviating from strict assay standards, debasement and plating of gold or silver on metals of lesser value. A situation was created whereby the worth of their coin was discounted internationally or, conversely, traded at a premium, thereby inflicting a mercurial rate of exchange upon the world. In an endeavour to correct these fluctuations and the ratio of gold to silver, numerous assay combinations and weight ratios came into being. Their application was only partially successful, as any attempt to regulate a bi-metallic currency artificially is inconsistent with its availability and production costs, as well as the supply of and demand for precious metals, which affects their current value.

Minting standards in disrepute

Exchange rates applied

Failure to regulate bi-metallic currency

Often, through the connivance of an issuing authority, a local premium was placed on the value of its own currency by refusing to accept foreign coin or summarily discounting it as payment for official debts, such as taxes, and by these manipulations made its minting activities more profitable. Sometimes coin lost its credibility through wear, debasement, deliberate clipping of metal from its edge, change of the status quo, or where the intrinsic value of bullion exceeded face value. The

Currency manipulations

24

issue was in these circumstances often withdrawn from circulation, melted down, assayed and re-struck. Hammered minting methods, as described, were principally unaltered until the sixteenth century AD. During the Renaissance the remarkable Leonardo da Vinci (1452 – 1519) recorded his design for a coin planchet machine capable of producing blanks of perfect roundness, uniform thickness and weight. *Da Vinci's planchet machine*

With the introduction of the rolling press, metal could be rolled to uniform width from which blanks were cut. In the mid-sixteenth century rollers each with several engraved dies were employed. The rolled blanks were passed between them, producing roller mill impressions of the dies simultaneously on obverse and reverse in long strips which were then cut into individual coins. The screw press, generally attributed to the Italian architect/medallist, Donato Bramante (1444 – 1514), overcame the problem of uneven striking by applying a uniform pressure to the coin blanks. The first mint master to use the screw press is thought to be the sculptor Benevenuto Cellini (1500 – 1571), who was appointed *Maestro delle stampe* by Clemente VII in 1529, and it is likely that he used the screw press shortly after his appointment. He describes it in his Trattato dell'Oreficeria of 1568. *Machine striking*

Baldassare Peruzzi (1481 – 1536), student of Bramante, also pioneered the design of the screw press during his term of office (1527 – 1535) as architect and later mint master of the Republic of Siena. Though no positive evidence of the existence of a screw press at the Siena mint is known, documentary evidence and drawings by Peruzzi exist, housed in the Gabinetto dei Disegni, Uffizi Gallery, Florence, and would support the theory,* that the screw press was well diffused in Italy before it became common in Germany and France circa 1550.

A screw press was purchased for the Cours des Monnaies from Max Schwab, Augsburg, in 1552.

The introduction (circa 1573) of a die collar produced coins *Die collar introduced*

* Nicholas Adams, American Numismatic Society. Museum Notes No. 23, 1978

with a uniform roundness while striking a legend and/or design on to the edge of the coin to prevent clipping. This was achieved by encircling the blank with a metal collar during striking.

The screw press was introduced into England in 1561 by the Frenchman, Eloye Mestrel, and was used until 1573. The unfortunate M. Mestrel was executed for alleged forgery on what was probably a trumped-up charge. The press was then discontinued by the Corporation of Moneyers, for fear of their skills becoming redundant. However in 1662, hammered coins were finally superseded by the use of the improved mill and screw press. *Coin press widely adopted*

The new machines revolutionized minting – rivalling hammered coins in consistency, even-striking, definition and productivity. The early screw press consisted of a rigid base and frame through the centre of which was a large vertical screw device on which a sturdy, long transverse bar was fixed, heavily weighted at each end. The press was operated by a team consisting of a setter, who sat in a well in front of the machine (with his head out of the path of the rotating transverse bar). His function was to position and change the planchets, while assistants turned the screw, aided by thongs or ropes attached to either side of the weighted bar. The mechanism would compress the dies together by its screw action, which proved superior to the hammering techniques. Later machines were adapted through gear systems to utilize horse and water power for the mill and screw process. In England, the Commonwealth period which followed saw the introduction of the machinery of a French engraver, Pierre Blondeau. He produced superb engraving, and struck coins of great beauty and technical competence. *New machines revolutionize coin making*

Use of screw press

Horse drawn mills

Blondeau's machine introduced in England

During the industrial revolution the steam press was invented for the striking of coins. This was the result of the partnership between Matthew Boulton (1728 – 1809) and James Watt (1763 – 1819), which was to prove most effective. *Boulton and Watt partnership invents steam press*

Pantograph in use   The pantograph, an instrument for the mechanical copying of a drawing or diagram, etc. on the same or an enlarged or reduced scale, made its appearance in Europe in the seventeenth century, and was used for the engraving of coin dies. It consisted of an arm that was used to trace an enlarged design, while at the other end a revolving engraving tool simultaneously cut an exact reduction of the original, to produce a hub from which working dies were made. This reduction device enabled the engraver to work on a scale several times greater than the size of the coin. The quality, artistry and charm of the old master moneyers was regrettably

Coins mass-produced lost to mass production with modern-day mints that churn out billions of coins annually throughout the world.

Coin types or symbols are devices struck on coins principally to guarantee their weight, purity (fineness) and value and to identify the status and origin of one coin from another. The incredible variety of coin types which has come down to us from antiquity, evidence of perpetual minting activities throughout the ages, provides the framework of numismatic study and appreciation. The motives for the choice of symbols are complex. Coin types were often heraldic symbols, applied to coinage as a signet of authority directly responsible for the coins' correctness: e.g. early coins from Ephesus bore the symbol of a stag with the inscription "I am the badge of Phanes". The device was often the city's badge, family crest, royal coat of arms, or mark of the magistrate personally responsible for the validity of the coin issue. The designs were based on considerations of religion, commemoration, decoration, imitation, commercial or political needs, and other diverse motives. Coins, mirrors of history, reflect statements of fact; in contrast to the writings of historians who often seek to impose their points of view. The value of coins as public documents was soon realised and exploited. Coins were often struck or overstruck as a propaganda medium to inform the populace of a victory or succession, as a manifesto, or act of defiance. Strong rivalry existed between the city states of the ancient world and in character with their national sentiments and with their love of aesthetics in general they pursued artistic and technical superiority, guarding their minting rights as tenaciously as their commercial and political autonomy. The artistic achievement, originality and inventiveness of the Greek world is well known. Regrettably, however, only a very small part of its art works are known to exist. It is rare that an art work is found from this period in its original condition. Copies and forgeries even from the later Greek periods often lack the spirit of the originals. Miraculously, however, numerous coins have survived over a period of two and a half thousand years; some in remarkable condition,

Coin Types

Symbols – signet of authority

Coins mirror history

Coins as public documents

Pursuit of artistic and technical superiority

Minting rights jealously guarded

Many ancient coins survive intact

little changed from the day they were struck. This has been made possible by their small size and duplication, assisted by the practice of hoarding (an inevitability in times of crisis or war, from which the hoarder often failed to survive or return from), and the ideal conditions under which some of the specimens were buried. Coins of noble metal have often survived without corrosion in less than favourable conditions. These factors have enabled us to feast our eyes on many of these masterpieces in their original state without the need for restoration, just as the artist would have wished.

Master seal/die engravers held in high regard

The master seal/die engravers were generally held in high regard and for good reason. We can but marvel at their superb sense of design, and skilful positioning of type (principal device) and symbol (ancillary device) within the confines of the planchet.

Coins appreciated and owned by the masses

The coins' artistic merits were appreciated and, because of the great number produced, possessed by the masses, unlike any other art form. Their aesthetic value was realised apart from their intrinsic worth.

Coins and their religious connotations

Wherever practically possible, art and pagan worship were closely interrelated. Temples in the ancient Greek world were vast storehouses of art treasures. These treasures often portrayed a deity, religious object or symbol, in honour of their gods. This trend became firmly established as is evident from their appearance on coin types. During the various reigns coin was used as a medium of deification. Until the fourth century

Portraits appear on coins

BC the occurrence of portraits on coins are practically unknown. From the sixth century BC Persian coinage bore a full figure of their king with bow and arrow, a type repeated in many areas of Persian influence. It is unlikely that, before the death of Alexander the Great, portraits on coins were anything more than a symbolic representation. His deified likeness made its appearance with the issue of a regular series following the fragmentation of his Empire. Kings and Roman emperors who adopted ruler cult as a means of political control used coins to advertise their divine associations. Busts on coins were to become commonplace to the extent that during the Roman Empire that followed an identifying legend encircling the portraits became necessary – the model on which our modern coinage is based. *Indentifying legends introduced*

The versatility of coinage beyond its obvious usage is manifold, some of its ancillary uses being: prizes for athletes and competitors at games; a medium for publicizing a noteworthy event (such as an alliance, diplomatic exchange, or visit of an eminent dignitary); and a means of promoting personal renown throughout colonies and dominions. In addition coins made excellent souvenirs. Occasionally by portraying items in which the city state traded, coin types and symbols served as ideal advertising media, enjoying wide circulation. *Versatility of coinage*

The role of coinage in archaeology is of added significance because coins can be arranged in chronological sequence through the information given by their inscriptions. *Coins' chronological significance in archaeology*

The legend (lettered inscription) on coins became commonplace as a municipal or national label, primarily to augment the type or portrait of a ruler, the authority of an issue, or to name the monetary magistrate responsible for its correctness. It was used on occasion to record the date of issue and the mark of denomination, to describe a type in whole or part, to elaborate on inscriptions, to commemorate an alliance or to record the die engraver's signature. Legends on coin appear in various forms: a complete inscription, an inscription interspersed with abbreviation, a letter or letters in monogram or initial marks. *Legends expounded*

The use of a secret code – privy mark (including mintmark/initial mark) – was sometimes incorporated in the overall design or the legend, on occasion in the form of heraldic or personal symbols. This served to aid the issuing authorities in guarding against forgeries, by establishing the chronological minting sequence (as early coins were not dated), or by giving the identity of the moneyer, and was sometimes used as a commercial control or trademark. *Mintmarks employed*

Counterfeits and Debasement

Forgery practised since antiquity

Saxon times

Becker, 19th century master forger

Motivation for counterfeiting and forgery

The malpractice of defrauding the public by tendering counterfeit coin as official issue is almost as old as coinage itself. Man was quick to exploit its possibilities, with all its inherent evils, as is testified by the anti-counterfeit laws of Athens in the sixth century BC.

Counterfeiting was rife during the Roman era and evidence of the forgery of coin during the Roman occupation was discovered at Halton Chesters, in England. In Saxon times, Aethelstan, King of Wessex (924 – 939 AD), introduced anti-forgery measures.

In Germany between 1815 and 1825 the brilliance of Karl Wilhelm Becker, master forger, came to the fore. It is said that Becker offered his coins as acknowledged copies and his works, some three hundred and fifty different specimens, eluded the detection of many numismatic experts. It is significant to note that only through the use of photography and the subsequent publication of photographs of Becker's coins (which enabled detailed comparisons to be made) was the full extent of his activities realised. His forgeries were in the main Greek, Roman and Medieval. He produced hand engraved dies, using genuine old coins of low numismatic value for the fabric, from which he prepared his blanks. He struck his coins with a heavy hammer to simulate ancient striking techniques and thereafter placed them in a container filled with iron filings which was attached to the axle of his carriage, in order to produce an aged finish on the coins.

The methods and activities of forgers and monetary opportunists have made their mark historically. This is a scourge which continues to be omnipresent in contemporary society.

There are several motivations for counterfeiting activities: greed, pursuance of dishonest profit, the satisfaction of the forger in passing off his work as genuine, and undermining an enemy's economy by large scale forgery and manipulation of its currency. During World War II, Germany (under the direction of S.S. Major Bernhard Kruger) printed counterfeit bank notes, operating from Sachsenhausen concentration camp. Its inmates were forced to produce millions of English bank notes, which the Germans used to secure war supplies and intelligence services. Counterfeit coins have also been used as a weapon to inflict commercial sabotage on rival trading nations.

Debasement was employed throughout the ages by issuing authorities in times of crisis, or even for lesser motives. Its practice was aggravated by the introduction of paper money, a new concept introduced in China during the T'ang dynasty (618 – 907 AD) to supplement the coinage which had become scarce. This concept was conveyed by Marco Polo on his return from China in the thirteenth century. He noted the daily use of paper money on his journey during the Yuan dynasty. Western introduction of paper money originated in Sweden in 1661, to augment the shortage of specie, and was moreover potentially useful as a means of preventing the irrecoverable gold lost through normal daily wear and tear of gold coins in circulation. *Debasement*

Introduction of paper money

Inflation, in the main a product of debasement, is not peculiar to our time – its ravages were experienced on many occasions throughout the ages. The effects of World War I precipitated a monetary crisis that ultimately forced most nations to abandon the gold standard (i.e. the convertibility of paper money for gold in specie). *Inflation product of debasement*

Gold standard abandoned

As attempted in the past, governments issue bank notes in excess of their backing (gold reserves) with which they endeavour, through legislation, to create additional reserves. The resultant debased fiat currency causes inflation; a temporary state of euphoria is reached and all known remedies become politically disastrous. Time is bought in the short term by injections of indiscriminate credit, handouts to curry favour with the electorate and printing a greater volume of bank notes, thereby widening the rift between the bank note issue and its gold backing. This feeds inflation, thereby eroding economic stability and confidence with alarming effect on the real worth of savings, fixed in- *Inflation erodes economic stability*

33

comes, pensions and the entire economic system. The tax collector at this point is obliged to impose additional punitive taxation to try to make sense of the inflated money (of little value) that is returned by the tax payer. This adds further fuel to the fire and ultimately rampant inflation stifles incentive, causing widespread dissatisfaction and demands for higher wages. In the economic vortex of despondency the public at large becomes the victim of misrepresentation, having to face the bleak realities of the inflationary/deflationary spiral. This is, of course, an over-simplification but it is hoped that it will suffice to illustrate the point.

Erosion of incomes and tax receipts

Punitive taxation stifles incentive

Throughout history the control of money, contrived by means outside the natural disciplines of specie, has succumbed to human frailty – for example, Winston Churchill's overvaluation of sterling in 1920. The introduction in 1970 by the International Monetary Fund of special drawing rights (SDRs), machinery for the arbitrary granting of credit against imaginary reserves of paper gold of no intrinsic value, is yet another contrived scheme in history aimed at the demonetisation of specie. Some notable failures of fiat money which ended in disaster were: its introduction during the Ming dynasty in the fifteenth century; **John Palmstruck's Kreditivedlar notes in Sweden in 1661; the attempt by John Law (a Scot) to save the French economy in 1716; the German economic disaster of the 1920s; and the Hungarian failure of 1946** – to name but a few.

Some examples noted

Counterfeit coin circulated in quantity would tend to have an effect similar to the undisciplined printing of paper money. In 405 BC Aristophanes said of the emergency money issued in Athens, "In our Republic bad citizens are preferred to good; just as bad money circulates whilst good money disappears." This has been the case throughout history. In the reign of Queen Elizabeth I of England, it is recorded that Sir Thomas Gresham explained this phenomenon to the Queen as the reason for the flight of gold from the realm, due to debased coin struck during the reign of her father, Henry VIII. This phenomenon became

Coin debasement and counterfeits

Gresham's Law

34

known as Gresham's Law: Bad money drives out the good.

The standards of counterfeits vary greatly, from crude replicas to masterpieces of deception that have on occasion deceived the experts. Allied to counterfeiting is the malpractice of removing small amounts of metal from coin and passing them off as full measure. This took the form of clipping, i.e. cutting or machining small slivers of metal from the edge of the coin. This practice has been prevented by the introduction of inscriptions (in either incuse or relief) circumscribing the edge, sometimes with the inclusion of an edge design or by the use of a milled rim.

Various standards of counterfeits

Allied malpractices

Precautions against malpractices

Rubbing or filing of coin was curbed by the inclusion of fine detail such as hairlocks, harp strings, etc., within a protected area of the design which served to indicate any appreciable signs of wear or removal. This indicator assisted in countering the practice of *sweating* – a method of removing gold by chemical reaction. Coin was laid in a glass vessel raised on three glass points. The vessel was then filled with aqua regia (a mixture of nitric and hydrochloric acids) which dissolves gold. This diminished the weight without producing an appreciable difference in the visual appearance of the coin, due to the uniform reaction.

Further precautions have been taken to minimise monetary malpractices and counterfeiting. Activities are restricted by the complexity of coin design, requiring the expert skills of craftsmanship. On occasion, coin is struck on specially prepared blanks, sometimes with the inclusion of privy marks (secret inscriptions). In some countries the disabilities of the blind are catered for in the design of contemporary coinage to enable them to differentiate between the various denominations through their sense of touch; this assists in preventing unscrupulous persons from giving them incorrect change.

The rise in popularity of vending machines brought with it other fraudulent practices such as the use of foreign coins, metal discs and other substitute objects. Despite the introduction of acceptor/rejector devices it became clear that a sophisticated means of countering the boundless ingenuity of the human mind was essential. As an answer special metals were developed which have a lower saturation magnetization than that of nickel. These metals are not used industrially nor are they commercially available. Their production is restricted to government controlled orders, as with the printing of bank notes. Nickel and cupro-nickel when used in laminates of various combinations and permutations provide a coin fabric which is discernible by modern magnetic acceptor/rejector devices – thus making positive detection of counterfeit coins possible. Mint authorities have set up a central register to avoid duplication of their specifications.

Anti-forgery devices are also applied to the printing of paper currency. Special paper, water marks, metal coding strips manufactured between the paper's fabric, special inks and complex designs of intricate and sharply defined illustrations are employed.

Laws of legal tender

Laws of legal tender, generally in use, specify the prescribed weight and tolerance (remedy) governing the acceptance of coin. Punishment of great severity has been meted out to counterfeiters as a deterrent, but the profitable felony continues with coins of noble metals or numismatic value. Counterfeiting or treatment of contemporary coins (usually mere tokens of value), has been curtailed and discrepancies today would have to be minimal requiring treatment of vast quantities of coin, which would negate the profitability of this ac-

Some revealing features of forgeries

tivity. The use of debased metal is bound to reveal itself by its incorrect weight, specific gravity, poor fabric, colour variance, etc. It was often the practice of counterfeiters in ancient times to plate or dip coins of base metal in either silver or gold to pass them off as coins of noble metal. To guard against this, suspect coins were violated by cutting

Methods of minimising coin's wear

them through. Another consideration is the wear factor which is minimised by the introduction of alloying elements to harden the metal. Alloys such as cupro-nickel, used in contemporary minting, are selected for their hardwearing properties, relative cheapness and resistance to corrosion. Modern coins are usually designed with an edge rim in relief protruding slightly above the surface of the coin type. This acts as a buffer to minimise abrasion when coins are stacked and to assist in withstanding the general wear and tear of circulation.

With the meteoric rise in coin prices and the ever-swelling ranks of the numismatic fraternity throughout the world, counterfeiters unleash their activities on the unsuspecting public at large, preying on the bargain hunter and those imprudent collectors and dealers who acquire coins from doubtful sources. On occasion, excellent and dangerous counterfeits have passed the scrutiny of experts and dealers of repute. To counter this problem, the International Association of Professional Numismatists (IAPN) founded the International Bureau for the Suppression of Counterfeit Coins in London, under the direction of Mr. E.G.V. Newman OBE, BSc, an internationally acknowledged expert. Mr Newman, who recently retired as Chemist and Assayer of the Royal Mint, has been actively concerned with counterfeits since 1953, and has prepared expert evidence in over 500 cases to date. The objectives of the Bureau are: *The IBSCC*

(i) to collect, edit, publish and circulate information on counterfeits, not only to members of the IAPN but also to other interested bodies and individuals;

(ii) to build up a data bank of information on counterfeits of both antique and current coins which will be available for use by members of the IAPN, by law enforcement authorities and by other institutions and interested individuals;

(iii) to arrange for the authentication of doubtful coins by experts and, where necessary, for their testing by scientific methods;

(iv) to work for changes in legislation in different countries which would make illegal the manufacture of counterfeits of both current and non-current coins of all countries and of

* Continued on page 40

left: 1794/10   x40

right: 1794/9   x40

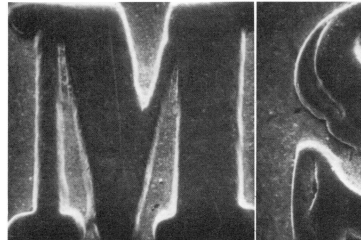
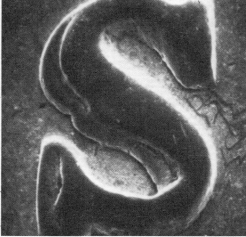

left: 1794/8   x90
60° tilt

right: 1794/7   x2K

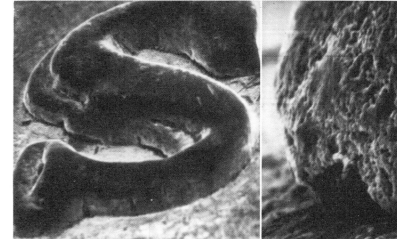

U.S.A. ONE DIME 1894 S (SILVER)

GENUINE
Weight: 2,5 ± 0,0972 grams
Fineness: silver, 900 ± 3 parts per 1 000
Specific gravity: 10,3 – 10,32
Diameter: 17,91 mm
Struck: ↑ ↓

COUNTERFEIT
REPORT
SEPTEMBER, 1978
No. 181

GENERAL: R.S. Yeoman, 27th Edition, p. 108 quotes the quantity minted as 24 and states that at a private sale in 1972 one such coin fetched $50 000.

THIS COIN (with transposed "S")
Weight: 2,4520 grams
Fineness: silver, approx. 900 parts per 1 000
Specific gravity: 10,30
Diameter: 17,81/17,82 mm

OBVERSE: Correct, slightly worn.

REVERSE: Correct (and slightly worn) except for the mint mark "S". This side shows that the coin is a common Philadelphia Mint (no mint mark) dime of 1894. An "S" has been sliced off a common San Francisco (mint mark "S") dime of another date and affixed to this piece. Twelve Scanning Electron Microscope photographs at magnifications of x40 to 2K (2 000) were taken of the "M" of "DIME" and the mint mark "S". Four are reproduced here, viz.,

1794/10: Showing the "M" and how its base flows into the table, i.e., there is no discontinuity between them.

1794/9: Showing the "S" and the discontinuity between its base and the table. Note the peculiar "doubling" of the left side of the "S" and what appear to be tool marks on the table in front of its top serif.

1794/8: Showing the "S", with the coin at 60° tilt.

1794/7: Showing where one small portion of the "S" meets the table: the base of the letter is discontinuous with, and the metal does not flow into, the table as with a genuine piece.

Simultaneous microprobe analyses showed the table and consequently the whole of the original coin to be 900 silver and, likewise, the "S" to be 900 silver; no evidence could be found of a brazing material between.

This coin was offered by an American to Spink & Son Ltd., for auction.

The Bureau would like to thank Mr Robin Keeley of the Metropolitan Police Forensic Science Laboratory for carrying out the Scanning Electron Microscopy and microprobe analyses, without which this report would not have been possible.

reproductions of coins which are not adequately marked as such; and

(v) to collaborate closely with the American Numismatic Association Certification Service and with other bodies in the furtherance of these aims.

The Bureau publishes a quarterly bulletin on counterfeits which is of high standard and includes many photographic illustrations, clearly indicating the defects, to aid the identification of counterfeits. Technical information, such as coins' dry weight, specific gravity, edge faults and other peculiarities are indicated. In rare cases, sophisticated tests are employed in reaching a decision as to the authenticity of a coin, such as X-ray fluorescence spectrometry and/or spectrography.

Several non-destructive methods of analysis and dating are now in use, employing the physical, nuclear and photographic sciences. Detailed reports are issued on a restricted basis. These reports are sent to members of the IAPN and are available on a subscription basis to numismatic and other academic institutions, government agencies, mints, police, banks, bullion merchants and dealers as well as collectors able to supply the required reference to the Board of Management of the IBSCC. The IBSCC does not grade items as to condition nor determine where the coins are produced as proof or otherwise, nor does it offer any estimate of value. It does not identify, contribute items, describe the criteria for determining that an item is a counterfeit or an altered piece, or recommend dealers or other authorities. The IBSCC and ANACS (American Numismatic Association Certification Service) are complementary and work closely together. The IBSCC strongly recommends that numismatists in North America wishing to avail themselves of an authentication service send both their North and South American coins to the ANACS, as that body has particular knowledge of American issues.

The existing series of coins is so profuse and complex that its incorporation is beyond the scope of any one book. The photographic plates represent a cross-section of coins spanning two and a half thousand years. The enlargements have been juxtaposed with photographs of the coins in their actual size and the accompanying notes are keyed with detailed line drawings. Facsimiles of the legends have been illustrated, expanded and translated.

Seals predate coins; examples together with their impressions illustrate the use of the incuse/embossed (negative/positive) technique. Each seal was unique and was used to append a symbol and/or signature to attest a tablet, document or object, to denote authority and as a mark of ownership and a method of preventing undetected access. Seals were made from semi-precious stones or other hardwearing and decorative materials and were often worn as amulets or jewellery.

Circa 2000 BC
MESOPOTAMIA
UR (Third Period)
Serpentine Cylinder Seal
Length: 33,5 mm
16 mm diameter
Effective area of
impression 47 x 30 mm

see page 51

The presentation scene depicts a deity, wearing a flounced robe and a head-dress, seated beneath a crescent moon, facing left, with one hand raised. A goddess approaches leading a worshipper by the hand. There are two vertical panels bearing symbols which have not been deciphered and it is possible that these have been recut in more recent times.

Circa 1700 BC
OLD BABYLONIAN
Serpentine Cylinder Seal
Length: 22 mm
13 mm diameter
Effective area of
impression 37 x 22 mm

A bearded god with a head-dress gestures towards a figure in a short robe and turban (probably a king). He stands facing the goddess Lama who has both hands raised. A worshipper in a striped robe and turban head-dress faces a bearded god who has an open skirt and head-dress and stands with one foot raised. He holds a symbol known as the rod with (seven) balls which has been associated with various deities, especially Adad and Shamash, and is flanked by symbols which have been interpreted in various ways: a ball and staff; libation

42

vessel; scales for weighing; a measuring rod and a hookah. Between the god and the king is a seven-pointed star and a fish.

The scarab shaped amulet, resembles the sacred beetle of the ancient Egyptians, and is carved on its underside in intaglio with a bull which has the beak of a bird. Its long tail extends to form the base line and the design is surrounded by a single line oval border.

Circa 1000 BC
SYRIA
"Egyptian Faience"
Scarab Length: 22 mm
Breadth 16,5 mm
Effective area of
impression 14 x 20 mm

43

Greek Coins The artistic achievements of the ancient Greek world are generally divided into seven chronological classifications:

700 – 480 BC PERIOD OF ARCHAIC ART

This period saw the beginning of the coin maker's art, during which time techniques in both the fabric and design were nurtured. The style was generally angular and crude, but with a certain archaic sensitivity peculiar to its age.

480 – 415 BC PERIOD OF TRANSITIONAL ART

This was a time of significant advance in die engraving and minting techniques. The result was refinement of detail in remarkably accurate portrayal of the human anatomy displaying greater freedom of movement. Both type and symbol were masterfully placed within the confines of the planchet. The incuse square design was refined to contain devices, ornamental quartering and inscriptions. This period produced some of the most intricate and delicately engraved coins ever struck. The engraving was executed with assured confidence; in high relief and with a strong sense of design, bold experimentation and attention to detail.

415 – 336 BC PERIOD OF FINEST ART

This was the pinnacle of the master die engraver's art when artistic heights in the cutting of dies and striking of coin were achieved, which to this day have not been surpassed. With an intensity of purpose and rivalry, the die engravers gave life to the metal for posterity. From their resounding hammer blows still echoes the age of artistic glory that was ancient Greece. So proud were these masters of their coin dies that they inscribed their works with minuscule signatures. The works of artists such as Kimon, Euainetos, Phyrgillos, and Eukleidas will be marvelled at for all time. This was a period of facing, three-quarter and profile heads, so magnificently produced that they radiate vitality, spirit, depth and personality that transcends more than two millennia. The development of the chariot group and the figure of Nike portrayed on the famed Syracusan Decadrachms explore all avenues of realism and perspective with ingenuity and delicacy, yet with forceful effect.

336 – 280 BC PERIOD OF LATER FINE ART

Some quite remarkable portraits appearing on coins of this period have, to quote Seltman (in his *Masterpieces of Greek Coinage*, page 88), "The face and eyes that can deal harshly with men that do evil, for here is terrible power with transcendent calm." The heads of deities were often substituted for those of mortal rulers. A predominance of increasingly lifelike seated figures on the reverse characterizes the period.

280 – 146 BC PERIOD OF THE DECLINE OF ART

This period saw the rise of the Hellenistic kings, and mainly regal issues were minted. With the defeat in 190 BC of Antiochus by the Romans, many Greek states regained their minting rights. They minted coin either in their own name, or by utilising the pattern of Alexander the Great, usually with the addition of their symbols and/or legends. One can easily differentiate between the original coinage of Alexander and those of later issues by their style, large dimensions and evidence of debasement. Owing to the dictates of the Macedonian kings there was no minting in Athens for about a century. Athenian mints restarted their coin making activities from about 220 BC, issuing their new style coinage in great quantity. In Italy most autonomous minting activities ceased with the advent of Roman silver coinage in 268 BC.

146 – 27 BC PERIOD OF CONTINUED DECLINE

This period marked the further decline of minting standards and the increased minting of bronze coin. Under Roman rule most of the Greek states were deprived of their right to coin money.

27 BC – 268 AD GREEK IMPERIAL PERIOD

With the advent of Roman domination minting activities were largely confined to Rome. Roman emperors in the eastern half of the Empire allowed a large number of states to mint bronze coin for special occasions only. These minting rights were rarely granted in the western half of the Empire however. The coinage of this period has become known as Greek Imperial (actually municipal). Typical of this period are types depicting temples and local officialdom.

The Republican and Imperial Roman eras followed that of Greece and produced a magnificent wealth of coinage spanning more than a thousand years. This significantly assisted in recording for posterity (with its own characteristic style), the fabric of Roman life on which much of modern civilisation is built. The portraits on many of their coins convey the spirit of the personalities that ruled throughout this period, sometimes with incredible realism; probing the depths of long forgotten aspirations, hope, pride, cruelty and achievement.

OBVERSE: The confronting foreparts of the lion and bull echo the gold repoussé work of the period.

560 – 546 BC
LYDIA
KING CROESUS
Gold Stater
8,10 grams
16 mm diameter

REVERSE: The conjoined incuse squares are of irregular size and plane.

This is probably one of the first gold coin types struck.

see pages 52, 53

OBVERSE: The ferocious lion's head in profile left, truncated with a vertical row of pellets, is within an incuse square.

Circa 500 – 450 BC
CYZICUS
Silver Diobol
1,32 grams
11 mm diameter
← *

REVERSE: The forepart of the winged boar, truncated with a row of pellets, is juxtaposed with a tunny fish which is positioned vertically.

Cyzicus was a Milesian colony on the southern shores of the Propontis (Marmara Sea – Turkey) which rivalled Byzantium in strategic and commercial importance.

see page 56

OBVERSE: The composite mythical creature is probably Phobos, personification of fear. This winged human male with facing torso and lupine/canine head and tail, in profile right, is half-kneeling and holds a tunny fish by its tail left.

Circa 500 BC
CYZICUS
Electrum Cyzicene Stater
16,13 grams
20 mm diameter

REVERSE: The incuse quadripartite square has individual gradient faces.

The electrum stater known as a Cyzicene, enjoyed wide fame and was characterized by the tunny fish (the city's badge) which contributed to the prosperity of the colony.

see pages 54, 55

*Die axis – see page 366

OBVERSE: The head of Dionysus, the god of wine, facing right, is garlanded with leaves.

The powerful yet benign portrayal of this deity is given added dimension by the subtle positioning of the beard in relation to the border of pellets.

REVERSE: Silenus, boon companion of Dionysus, is portrayed as a nude squatting ithyphallic satyr with a beard, horse's ears and tail and holds a kantharos (wine cup) left. The legend is positioned in an arched formation in the upper field and is within a circular border of pellets.

Circa 450 BC
NAXOS (Sicily)
Silver Drachma
4,34 grams
18 mm diameter
→

see page 57

 OF THE NAXIANS

This masterpiece ascribed to the celebrated engraver now referred to as the Aetna Master is executed with anatomical perfection, scintillating vitality and animal magnetism. The impish reveller is brilliantly posed in semi-profile with splayed legs and a skilful foreshortening of the right foot. He is supporting himself with a straight arm on a flat hand which lends balance to his "drinking arm", cleverly posed in suspended animation. The male attributes of this well-endowed satyr are accentuated through an original interplay of shapes and a strong sense of design.

OBVERSE: The head of Athena, patron goddess of Athens, facing right, is adorned with a necklace and pearl earring(s). Her hair is fashioned with scalloped locks and falls over her forehead and temples, and from under the neck piece of her crested helmet which is embellished with olive leaves and a floral scroll. The coin is struck in high relief and is portrayed with superb realism.

REVERSE: The owl (*Athene noctua*, still found in Greece) with facing head and staring eyes, stands inclined to the right. In the top left corner is an olive sprig with a distant decrescent moon positioned between it and the owl. The coin has an incuse square field and the legend is positioned vertically right.

Circa 440 BC
ATHENS
Silver Tetradrachm
17,15 grams
25 mm diameter
→

 ATHE(NIAN)

Athens, great cultural and political centre, had naval power as its corner stone which, together with the abundant silver deposits mined within its borders at Laurium, enhanced its might. An articulated range of denominations was minted which became internationally accepted and respected for its consistency in weight and fineness. These issues, though often crudely engraved and carelessly struck, were copious, as is evident from the numerous hoards found in and beyond the Greek world.

see pages 58, 67

Circa 415 – 403 BC
CATANA (Sicily)
Silver Tetradrachm
16,58 grams
26 mm diameter
←

see pages 68, 77

OBVERSE: The laureate head of Apollo facing, with the signature of the master die engraver positioned vertically in the field right, is within an engrailed border.

ΗΡΑΚΛΕΙΔΑΣ HERACLEIDAS

Apollo, in art, is personified as idealized youth, yet with mature manly beauty. He is associated with music, archery, prophecy, medicine, care of livestock and the higher ideals of civilization and its principles. This signed masterpiece is the work of the celebrated die engraver Heracleidas. His powerful study is superbly engraved in high relief and is subtly inclined left, the forehead gently tapers upwards to accentuate the deep-set piercing eyes. It is charged with vitality and confronts the viewer from any angle with terrible power yet with serene and youthful charisma. The luxuriant hair is masterfully stylized in a juxtaposition of wild and ordered locks.

REVERSE: This galloping quadriga, left, is met by Nike, the winged goddess of Victory, who, hovering above the reins, is about to crown the victorious charioteer. Below the exergual ground line is the legend and a fish.

ΚΑΤΑΝΑΙΩΝ OF THE CATANIANS

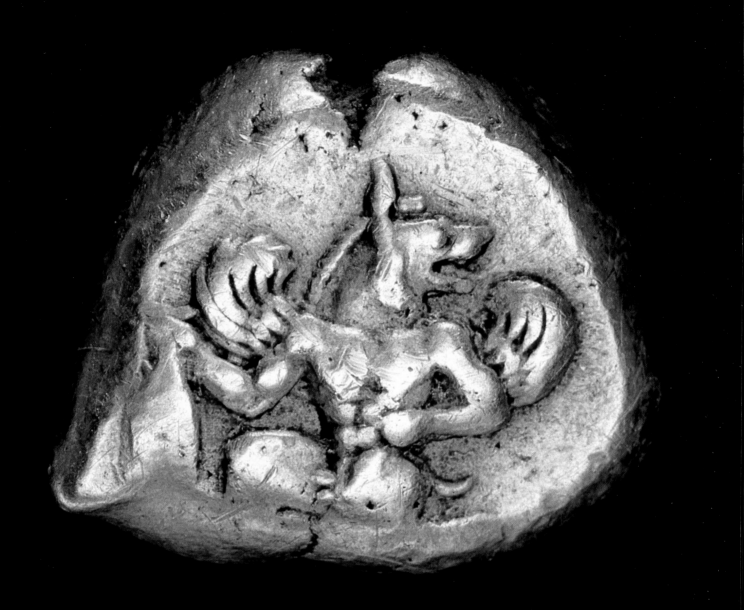

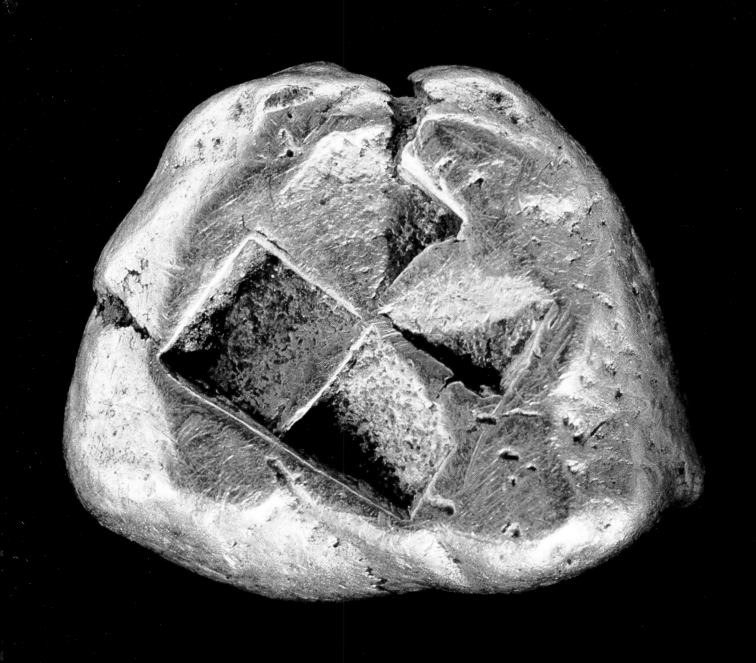

OBVERSE: A victorious quadriga gallops to the left, the charioteer holds the reins in his left hand and with his outstretched right arm wields a kentron (rod). Nike flies towards him with both arms extended and holds a laurel wreath with which she is about to crown him. The quadriga is engraved with elegance, harmony and power; yet has ordered vitality, intensified by the skilful placement of the meandering tail of the horse.

Beneath the prominent exergual ground line is a panoply ranged on steps, comprising a cuirass, flanked by a pair of greaves with a shield to the left and a crested helmet to the right. The legend appears below the cuirass.

 PRIZES

REVERSE: The head of Arethusa, water nymph daughter of Ceres, faces left. Struck in high relief, she is adorned with a pearl necklace and earring(s) and her luxuriant hair is contained within a sphendone and bound with an ampyx bearing the initial K(imon). Four shimmering, lively-looking dolphins within a pearled border surround her. The dolphin beneath bears the signature of Kimon and is skilfully positioned as an adjunct to soften the truncation. The elegance of this peerless nymph is stunning.

 OF THE SYRACUSANS

It is likely that these issues formed the main coinage of the tyrant Dionysius and may have been distributed as prizes to the athletes at the Assinarian Games celebrated by the people of Syracuse from 412 BC onwards to commemorate their victory over the Athenians. The armour shown in the exergue is generally thought to have been the spoils of that war and might have been presented as prizes at the games.

Circa 405 BC
SYRACUSE (Sicily)
Silver Decadrachm
43,07 grams
33 mm diameter

see pages 78, 79

Circa 390 BC
SYRACUSE (Sicily)
Gold 100 Litrae =
two Silver Decadrachm
5,80 grams
14 mm diameter
Dies by Euainetos
↘

see pages 80, 81

OBVERSE: The head of Arethusa in high relief faces left with her hair elegantly coiffured and held in an ampyx and a sphendone, ornamented with two stars each with eight rays. She wears a necklace and triple pendant earring(s) and has a third star behind her neck. The legend is positioned vertically to the left.

ΣΥΡΑΚ[ΟΣΙΩΝ] OF THE SYRACUSANS.

REVERSE: The nude youthful Hercules (Herakles), kneeling on an undulating ground line, is strangling the Nemean lion. He is accomplishing one of the twelve labours assigned by Eurystheus to regain his freedom, symbolic of man's struggle in attaining self realisation.

The concentric arrangement is ingeniously composed to accommodate the heroic contest on the minuscule circular planchet.

"So from Nemea's den Alcides (Herakles) strode,
The lion's yellow spoil around his shoulder flo'ed."

Flaccus

OBVERSE: The *Silphium* plant with the name of the city B – A/P – K – A – I arranged between its leaves, within an engrailed border.

B A
P K   BARCE
A I

This famous plant (a form of Asafoetida, now extinct) was in great demand throughout the ancient world for its medicinal properties, the perfume extracted from its flowers and as a vegetable.

Circa 360 BC
BARCE,
CYRENAICA
North African
Greek colony (Libya)
Silver Tetradrachm
12,70 grams
29 mm diameter
↓

REVERSE: The facing head of Zeus Ammon, the principal deity of Cyrenaica, with a beard, drooping moustache and the ram's horns of Ammon is within a concentric border with an inner pattern of denticles. The legend appears in the lower field left and right.

A K E [S] I O S   HEALER

This remarkable portrait has tragic eyes that confront, transfix and mesmerize with awesome power.

Zeus, weather god of Indo-European origin, was believed to have dominated the skies and was revered as the guardian of morality, law and order. He was associated by the Greeks with the cult of Ammon, originating from the ancient Egyptian ram-god of Thebes Amo[u]n-ra. This cult spread in the classical period not only to Cyrenaica but also to mainland Greece, in part because of the reputation of the oracle of Ammon at Siwah in the Western Desert.

see pages 82, 83

OBVERSE: The youthful head of Apollo in high relief faces right and his curls are bound with a laurel wreath.

⧚ ΦΙΛΙΠΠΟΥ OF PHILIP

359 – 336 BC
MACEDONIA
PHILIP II
Father of Alexander
the Great
Gold Stater
8,85 grams
18 mm diameter

REVERSE: The charioteer drives a biga and with his arm extended wields a kentron. A trident symbol is positioned horizontally under the raised front legs of the horses, which gallop on an exergual ground line, and below is the legend. The group probably depicts Philip's victory in a chariot race at the Olympic Games.

see page 84

OBVERSE: The facing Gorgon was a terrible mythical monster who had snakes instead of hair and eyes which could transform people into stone. The humanized portrayal is a remarkable microcosm of Greek art.

Circa 350 – 333 BC
SELGE
principal city of Pisidia
Silver Obol
0,82 grams
10 mm diameter

REVERSE: Athena, with head in profile right, wears a crested helmet and to the left is an astragalos symbol (knuckle bones used for gaming). The astragalos may be a pun on the name Selge.

see page 93

OBVERSE: The head of Athena, facing right, is adorned with pendant earring(s) and her undulating locks flow from beneath the neckpiece of her Corinthian helmet which is embellished with a serpent and a crest.

This exquisite face struck in high relief stands out as a monumental example of the die engraver's art. There is no symbol by which the mint may be determined and this is unusual. Athena, goddess of wisdom, patroness of agriculture, industry and the arts, guided men through war, gaining victory by prudence, courage and perseverance.

336 – 323 B.C.
MACEDONIA
ALEXANDER THE
GREAT
Gold Stater
8,58 grams
18 mm diameter
→

REVERSE: Winged Nike stands left, attired in a long chiton. She holds out a laurel wreath in her right hand and a stylis in her left. The stylis was a small mast and the symbol may indicate Alexander's concern with building up a powerful fleet. She is flanked by the legend placed vertically on either side.

see pages 94, 95

   OF ALEXANDER, THE KING

OBVERSE: Ptolemy I Soter, facing right, is wearing a diadem in his hair and the aegis of Zeus around his neck.

REVERSE: Alexander the Great, deified and semi-nude, is driving a quadriga of elephants to the left. He holds a thunderbolt in his right hand. Above is the legend and below the exergual ground line is the monogram.

304 – 283 BC
EGYPT
PTOLEMY I SOTER
Gold Stater
7,10 grams
18 mm diameter

see pages 96, 97

OF KING PTOLEMY

It is significant that this Ptolemaic issue was the first regular coinage struck in ancient Egypt and was the first known to portray the actual likeness of a ruler. This effigy of Ptolemy I dominated the coins throughout the dynasty which he founded in 305 BC and which continued until the death of Cleopatra in 30 BC. He was a Macedonian soldier, an administrator, a historian of distinction, and companion of Alexander the Great, after whose death he gained Egypt as his share of the conquest, and developed Alexandria as its new capital.

OBVERSE: Alexander the Great, deified as Zeus Ammon, faces right and wears a diadem and the horn(s) of Ammon in this expressive portrait.

REVERSE: Athena, enthroned left, wears a long chiton and a crested Corinthian helmet. In the palm of her right hand she supports Nike who holds a wreath above the legend which is placed vertically left. Her left arm rests on a shield, embossed with a lion's head, which is propped up against her throne. There is a spear diagonally to her right and the remainder of the legend is in the field behind her.

305 – 281 BC
THRACE
KING LYSIMACHUS
(Posthumous issue of
Alexander)
Gold Stater
8,52 grams
18 mm diameter
Minted at Pella
circa 286 – 281 BC
←

There is a symbol below her extended hand and the letter K in the exergue.

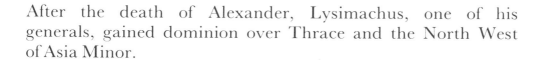

KING LYSIMACHUS

After the death of Alexander, Lysimachus, one of his generals, gained dominion over Thrace and the North West of Asia Minor.

The design of this reverse probably provided the model for the Roman Sestertius of Antoninus Pius, and almost certainly the inspiration for the Britannia design which appears on British coins from the reign of Charles II.

see page 98

Circa 200 BC
CLAZOMENAE
ALEXANDER
THE GREAT
(Posthumous issue)
Silver Tetradrachm
16,79 grams
33 mm diameter

↖

see page 115

OBVERSE: The head of Herakles is in a helmet made from the scalp of the Nemean lion. The Macedonian kings claimed to be descendants of their hero whose famous first labour made an appropriate theme for this enormous series which continued to be minted for centuries after Alexander's death.

REVERSE: Zeus, enthroned, facing left and semi-nude, supports a sceptre with his left arm and holds a confronting eagle on the outstretched palm of his right hand. In the field left is a winged forepart of a boar. The boar's head was the emblem of this Ionian city. Below is the monogram and on the right is the legend positioned vertically.

 ΑΛΕΞΑΝΔΡΟΥ   ALEXANDER'S

After the Macedonian victory over the Greeks, Philip brought Aristotle to Macedonia to educate his son Alexander. At twenty years of age Alexander seized his right to succession, crushed the Greek states which planned his annihilation, and led a unified army of Macedonians and Greeks to victory over the Persians. Alexander's conquests, reaching as far as India, are legend. He died at the age of 32 and his vast but troubled kingdom was fragmented and taken over by his generals.

66

OBVERSE: The conjoined profile heads are a bearded male laureate, left, and a female with a diadem, right. Possibly Philonome and Tenes.

REVERSE: The twinheaded axe, probably a symbol of Dionysus, has a bunch of grapes to the left and a facing owl to the right below. There is a monogram to the left of the grapes, and above the heads of the axe is the legend, all within a laurel wreath.

   OF THE PEOPLE OF TENEDOS.

This obverse type, though not peculiar to Tenedos, appears on its coinage from about 550 to 470 BC and the design provided the model for the Janiform head of the early Roman bronze Aes Grave issues.

Circa 160 BC
TENEDOS
Silver Tetradrachm
15,96 grams
33 mm diameter
↑

see pages 116, 117

Coinage was relatively undeveloped at the time of Rome's ascendancy during the fourth and third centuries BC. Primitive Italian currency had consisted of uncoined pieces of bronze, known as Aes Rude; their Roman successors, called Aes Signatum, remained very heavy, but were cast with designs (e.g. elephant/sow). It has been suggested that these unwieldy pieces were made as donatives to troops. They weighed approximately five Asses, and are probably contemporary with the first truly coin-like issues of the Romans, which began in the early decades of the third century BC. The bronze coins, still cast, but now round, bore a mark of value for the first time; the principal denomination, the As, equalled the Roman pound (libra) about 325 grams. This coinage, which we know as Aes Grave, is best exemplified by the issue showing on the obverse Janus bifrons and the mark of value, and on the reverse the prow of a galley and the mark of value. Multiples and divisions of the As were also issued. During this period the first Roman silver coinage was introduced, probably to pay for the Pyrrhic war of 280–275 BC. The models for these Didrachms, or Staters, were the Greek coins of Rome's southern neighbours and are sometimes termed "Romano-Campanian". The first type shows Mars' head/horse's head with the inscription ROMANO, and many of the other early Didrachms have horse types. An exception, at the start of the first Punic war is an issue with the head of Diana on the obverse and Victory on the reverse. Gradually, the Greek model gave way to coins of more markedly Roman character, such as the quadrigatus issues which had on the obverse a Janiform head and on the reverse a quadriga driven by Victory, with the legend ROMA (circa 235 BC). This was replaced by the Victoriatus, but of greater significance was the introduction of the silver Denarius (circa 211 BC), a denomination which formed the cornerstone of both Republican and Imperial coinage. It was accompanied by bronze, struck rather than cast. Gold, however, was struck only in times of war or emergency, and did not form part of the regular coinage until Imperatorial times.

Roman Coins

OBVERSE: The head of Brutus, facing right, has the legend positioned vertically, left and right, and is encircled with a laurel wreath.

BRVTVS IMP[ERATOR]*

BRUTUS, THE GENERAL

REVERSE: The composite naval and military trophy has two prows, a tiller, a panoply, and the letter L between the crossed spears. The dagger top left is probably a propaganda device which symbolizes Brutus's involvement in the patriotic conspiracy which culminated in the assassination of Julius Caesar on the Ides of March 44 BC. The legend is vertically positioned to the left, CASCA, and to the right, LONGVS, and the coin is encircled with a border of pellets.

CASCA LONGVS

This remarkable coin reveals a sensitive, earnest Brutus, a man of independent spirit. He was an effective man of action, inclined to study, contemplation and literary pursuits.

*A title traditionally given to successful generals when they were awarded a triumph

42 BC
GREECE
BRUTUS,
MARCUS IUNIUS
QUINTUS CAEPIO
Gold Aureus
8,12 grams
21 mm diameter
Struck 43 – 42 BC
Issued conjointly with
Casca Longus co-
inspirator (the envious
Casca of Shakespeare's
Julius Caesar)
↑

see page 118

OBVERSE: This cruciform pattern is comprised of crescents, ornaments and pellets, with laurel as its principal device. The design was probably influenced by the Macedonian Staters of Philip (see page 62) which were struck profusely in Europe. The degeneration of this type appeared on Gaulish Staters that were introduced into Britain after the first Belgic invasion, circa 75 BC. As a result the features of Apollo's laureate head became obscure and the original design was lost to the die engravers of the Catuvellauni, and retrogressed into an ornamented cruciform pattern.

REVERSE: A charming spirited horse gallops to the right. Above it is a looped ornament with a pellet on either side and beneath it is a circle with eight triangular radial projections.

The Catuvellauni, a warrior people, occupied the approximate area of Bedfordshire, Hertfordshire, Huntingdonshire and Cambridgeshire, with sections of Buckinghamshire, Essex, Northamptonshire, Oxfordshire and Suffolk, and were probably the most powerful and influential tribe in Britain at that time. One of their subsequent rulers, Cunobelin, was styled by the Roman writer, Suetonius, *Rex Britanniorum*.

Circa 40 – 20 BC
BRITAIN
CATUVELLAUNI
TRIBE
Gold Stater
5,89 grams
15 mm diameter
From the Waddon Chase
hoard found at Narbury
in the parish of
Little Horwood,
Buckinghamshire

see page 119

OBVERSE: This laureate head of Nero in profile right, is magnificently coiffured, has an undulating orbicular tipped truncation and is encircled by the legend and a border of pellets.

NERO CLAUDIUS CAESAR AUGUSTUS GERMANICUS PONTIFEX MAXIMUS, HOLDER OF TRIBUNICIAN POWER, HAILED IMPERATOR, FATHER OF THE FATHERLAND, HIGH PRIEST

REVERSE: Nero is mounted on a charger and holds a couched lance profile right, and is accompanied by his mounted Praetorian prefect who shoulders a pike. The letters SC appear on either side in the field and below the exergual ground line is the legend. The coin is surrounded by a border of pellets.

BY DECREE OF THE SENATE   A MANOEUVRE

54 – 68 AD
ROME
NERO
Bronze Sestertius –
orichalcum, an alloy
of copper and zinc
27,05 grams
35 mm diameter
Minted in Rome
64 – 66 AD
↓

see pages 130, 131

In 54 AD Nero became Emperor. He was egotistical, assertive, treacherous and extravagant, which made him most unpopular, as did the rumours that he deliberately started the great fire that destroyed half of Rome. His excesses and extensive wars forced him to depreciate his coinage. Nero had a great passion for the arts and horsemanship which is mirrored in this splendid coin.

OBVERSE: The holy Temple vessel with a pearled rim (9 pearls to view) has a stem with a conical base which has an orb at its apex and a horizontal stand on angular feet. Above are the letters:

שקל ישראל

YEAR 2   SHEKEL (OF) ISRAEL

i.e. sh (enat) b (et), referring to the second year of freedom. The coin is surrounded by the legend within an invected border of pellets.

REVERSE: The triple stemmed branch of budding pomegranates is executed with simple beauty and fine style in high relief. It is surrounded by ancient Hebrew calligraphy which appears to repeat the pomegranate blossom motif at the ends of the letters and is encircled by an invected border of pellets. The pomegranate, a symbol of Israel, was one of the celebrated products of Palestine. It was used as a temple decoration and was associated with rain and fertility.

ירושלים הקדושה

JERUSALEM THE HOLY

66 – 70 AD
PALESTINE
THE JEWISH WAR
AGAINST ROME
Silver Shekel*
14,5 grams
22 mm diameter
4 mm depth
Struck in Jerusalem
during the second year of
freedom from Roman
domination 67 – 68 AD

see pages 132, 133

The Jews persistently refused to bow to Rome and their opposition to interference with their religious principles and way of life led to many uprisings. In May 66 AD, amid heavy losses, the Jews drove most of the Roman forces from Palestine. Nero was obliged to act decisively and to send his finest general Vespasian with a large force to check this dangerous precedent which threatened to undermine the domination of Rome.

*Early mention of the Shekel in the Bible *(Exodus XXX.13)* refers to the (silver) unit of weight which formed part of the Babylonian sexagesimal system

OBVERSE: The laureate bust of Domitian, in profile right, is surrounded by the legend and an engrailed border. The dominant personality of this ruthless tyrant is skilfully portrayed by placing effective accent on his powerful neck. This has been achieved by generous proportions, sculptural quality and the undulating flared truncation.

IMP[ERATOR] CAES[AR] DOMITIANVS AVG[VSTVS] GERM[ANICVS],P[ONTIFEX] M[AXIMVS] TR[IBVNICIAE] P[OTESTATIS] XII

81 – 96 AD
ROME
DOMITIAN
Silver Denarius
3,09 grams
19 mm diameter
Struck in Rome 93 AD

↓

IMPERATOR CAESAR DOMITIANUS AUGUSTUS, GERMANI-CUS, PONTIFEX MAXIMUS HOLDER OF TRIBUNICIAN POWER FOR THE TWELFTH YEAR

REVERSE: The standing figure Minerva, his chosen patroness, facing left, is draped in a chiton and wears a crested Corinthian helmet. She holds a spear in her left hand and a thunderbolt in her right, behind at her feet stands a shield. She is surrounded by the legend and an invected border.

see page 120

IMP[ERATOR] XXII CO[N]S[VL] XVI CENS[OR] P[ERPETVVS] P[ATER] P[ATRIAE]

HAILED IMPERATOR TWENTY TWO TIMES, CONSUL SIXTEEN TIMES, CENSOR FOR LIFE, FATHER OF THE FATHERLAND

When Domitian succeeded Titus in 81 AD he was an embittered and complex man and after the rebellion of Antonius Saturninus in 88 AD became increasingly ruthless, tyrannical and extravagant and his total domination broke the spirit of the Senate. He tried to impose the refinements of Greek culture on the unwilling Romans and made concerted efforts as a censor to raise the standard of morality which was not in keeping with the sensuality of his private life.

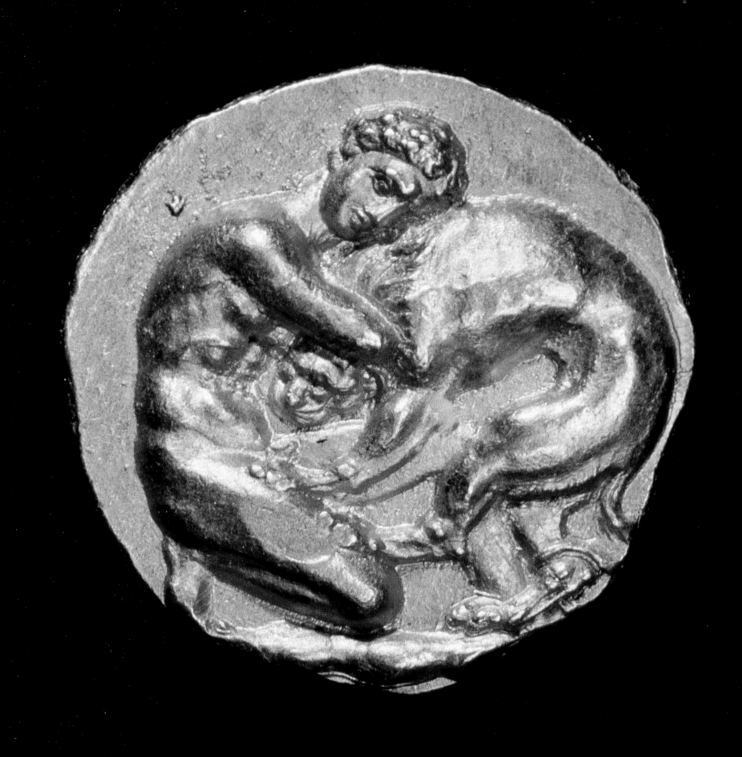

OBVERSE: The bust of Hadrian in profile, left, is draped and portrays him with luxuriant hair, a beard and a moustache, flanked by the legend and surrounded by a border of pellets.

HADRIANUS AUGUSTUS

REVERSE: Hadrian, with couched lance and robes flying, rides on a spirited charger which is poised on a short exergual ground line. He is flanked by the legend and encircled by a border of pellets.

THRICE CONSUL, FATHER OF THE FATHERLAND

This candid, pensive portrayal on the obverse is remarkable as is the vitality of the equestrian group with its minuscule likeness of Hadrian.

Hadrian was a most capable emperor and devoted his life to the cause of the Empire, widely popularizing his policies through his coin issues. His reign was relatively humane, popular and disciplined, but for the widespread repressive measures against the Jews, culminating in the destruction of the temple at Jerusalem.

117 – 138 AD
ROME
HADRIAN, PUBLIUS
AELIUS HADRIANUS
Gold Aureus
7,44 grams
20 mm diameter
Minted in Rome
128 – 138 AD
↓

see pages 134, 135

132 – 135 AD*
PALESTINE
THE BAR KOCHBA
WAR
Silver Tetradrachm
14,34 grams
26 mm diameter
3,5 mm depth
↑

see page 129

OBVERSE: The façade of the Temple at Jerusalem is shown as an architrave on four ribbed columns with capitals on a base of ashlars, eleven to view. The portable Ark of the Covenant which housed the Torah is centrally positioned and viewed from between the central pillars; the Torah scrolls are visible on a shelf. Above the architrave is a meander line. The legend is positioned vertically on either side of the Temple and the coin is encircled by a pearled border.

לחרות ירושלם

TO THE FREEDOM OF JERUSALEM

REVERSE: The lulav (palm branch) comprised of palm, myrtle and willow bound together is shown with the etrog (citron) to the left. These symbols are associated with water libation at the feast of Sukkot, which commemorates the sojourn of the Jews in the wilderness before reaching the Promised Land. The symbols are encircled by the legend and a pearled border.

שמ/עון

SHIMON/SIMON

Sixty-two years after the destruction of the second Temple the Jews engaged the Roman forces again. They were led by Rabbi Akiva and the military hero and civil leader Shimon Bar Kochba (Kosiva). They refused to concede the loss of the Temple and Hadrian's imposition of Roman culture was an intolerable prospect to the Jews who, with astonishing success, defeated the Romans. The Romans eventually amassed a considerable force against the Jews in 135 AD, and they were over-run and Jerusalem was destroyed.

*Striking ascribed to 134 – 135 AD, third year of freedom from Roman domination. Probably overstruck on a debased Tetradrachm of Antioch

OBVERSE: The embossed wreath has three berries between each of the leaves which are edged with dots. The leaf at 12 o'clock has a simple raised outline. The legend is centrally positioned within (in two lines) and the coin is encircled by a pearled border (traces of the Roman inscription visible). The letters are cast in the wrong order, viz:

and should read: שמעון

שמע/עון   SHIMON/SIMON

REVERSE: The fluted Temple vessel has a pearled band, a single handle and a narrow spout and base. To the right is a palm branch. Romanoff suggests in his book *Jewish Symbols on Ancient Jewish Coins* (pp. 29, 30) that these symbols were associated with water libation at the Festival of Sukkot. The coin is encircled by the legend and a pearled border.

לחרות ירושלם

TO THE FREEDOM OF JERUSALEM

132 – 135 AD*
PALESTINE
THE BAR KOCHBA
WAR
Silver Denarius
3,27 grams
18 mm diameter
↗

see page 136

*Overstruck on a Roman Denarius and ascribed to 134 – 135 AD, the third year of freedom from Roman domination

OBVERSE: The draped bust of Faustina, in profile facing right, is richly adorned with a diadem, pearl head-dress and earring(s) and is flanked by the legend and surrounded by a border of pellets. The stress marks which are evident on this specimen are caused by imperfect striking and co-incidentally provide the appropriate setting for this severe dignified matron whose portrait is infused with added vitality by the illusion thus created.

DIVA FAVSTINA   THE DEIFIED FAUSTINA

141 AD, Following
ROME
FAUSTINA, ANNIA
GALERIA, THE ELDER
Silver Denarius
3,25 grams
17 mm diameter
Posthumous issue struck
during the reign of her
husband Antoninus Pius
↑

REVERSE: Ceres wearing a diadem stands draped left. She holds a staff in her left hand, and ears of corn in her right. She is flanked by the legend and encircled within a border of pellets.

AVGVSTA   AUGUSTA

When Faustina died she was honoured by her devoted husband who struck extensive consecration issues on which she is depicted as numerous goddesses.

see page 145

88

OBVERSE: The draped bust, in profile left, of Antoninus Pius has a beard, luxuriant hair and a moustache and is surrounded by the legend and a border of pellets, partially apparent as a serrated pattern.

ANTONINUS PIUS AUGUSTUS, FATHER OF THE FATHERLAND, HOLDER OF TRIBUNICIAN POWER FOR THE SIXTEENTH YEAR

REVERSE: Antoninus Pius is draped in a toga and stands on a short exergual ground line, inclined to the left. He holds a globe in the outstretched palm of his right hand and is flanked by the legend and a border of pellets.

CO[N]S[VL] IIII   FOUR TIMES CONSUL

There is quiet strength and candour in this portrayal of the emperor. Antoninus Pius (Devout) was a title conferred on him by the Senate. He won the respect and recognition of Hadrian for his scruples, integrity and sterling qualities, and assumed power during Hadrian's last ailing months. His rule was tranquil, judicious, ordered and prosperous. He was married to Faustina and was a modest, simple living, disciplined man who liked harmony, helped numerous communities and built many public projects, yet through prudence he was able to cut public expenditure to the extent that left 675 million Denari in the treasury on his death in 161 AD.

138 – 161 AD
ROME
ANTONINUS PIUS,
TITUS AURELIUS
FULVUS BOIONIUS
Gold Aureus
7,34 grams
20 mm diameter
Struck in Rome
153 – 154 AD
↓

see page 146

161 – 169 AD
ROME
LUCIUS VERUS,
L. CEIONIUS
COMMODUS

Gold Aureus
7,28 grams
20 mm diameter
Struck in 162 AD

↓

see pages 155, 156

OBVERSE: The bust of Verus, in profile right, has luxuriantly coiffured hair in tight curls, a beard and moustache and a draped cuirass. The legend and an engrailed border surround him.

IMP[ERATOR] CAES[AR] L[VCIVS] VERVS AVG[VSTVS]

IMPERATOR CAESAR LUCIUS VERUS AUGUSTUS

REVERSE: Verus, with draped cuirass and tilted lance, is mounted on a trotting vivacious steed adorned with a collar, with three pellets to view, on a short exergual ground line, surmounted by an invected border and the legend.

PROFECTIO AVG[VSTI] TR[IBVNICIAE] P[OTESTATIS] II CO[N]S[VL] II

DEPARTURE OF THE AUGUSTUS (FOR THE EAST), HOLDER OF TRIBUNICIAN POWER FOR THE SECOND TERM; TWICE CONSUL

Verus was made co-emperor by his adopted elder brother, Marcus Aurelius, but though he campaigned in the East with some success his administration was poor. He was indulgent, pleasure loving, weak and characterless, which has been successfully portrayed by the die engraver. The characterisation on the reverse is humourously presented by his equestrian posture and vivacious steed.

OBVERSE: The bust of Diocletian, in profile right, with beard, moustache and hair with dapper trim, has ties dangling from the diadem. The truncation is flamboyantly styled and the bust is flanked by the legend and is within a pearled border.

DIOCLETIANUS AUG[VSTVS]

DIOCLETIANUS AUGUSTUS

REVERSE: The tetrarchy (four co-emperors) flanks the latticed arched gate of a fortification, the ramparts of which have eight turrets to view. The group is inclined with humble posture towards a sacrificial tripod positioned before the arch – a statement of tetrarchic unity. They are flanked by the legend and surrounded by a pearled border.

VIRTVS MILITVM

THE VALOUR OF THE TROOPS

284 – 305 AD
ROME
DIOCLETIAN,
GAIUS AURELIUS
VALERIUS
DIOCLETIANUS
Silver Argenteus
3,47 grams
18 mm diameter
Struck 293 – 294 AD

Diocletian was a bold administrator, statesman, reformer and general, and he transformed the Empire. Faced with a serious frontier situation and government dissension he adopted a policy of divide and rule, and formed the famous tetrarchy by dividing the Empire between himself, Maximianus, Constantinus Chlorus and Galerius, but it was only successful while bound by his dominance. Diocletian introduced important reform by separating civil from military control and he undertook a massive development of defensive construction on all frontiers, increasing the strength of his army, placing a great burden on the coffers of the empire. In an attempt to bolster state reserves, he minted large quantities of debased coin. Its effect sparked off a wave of inflation. In order to counter the return of the debased coin to his exchequer he introduced a system of inflation-linked taxation, which was revised at 15-year intervals. He tried in vain to establish a unified debased currency but was not able

see pages 157, 158

to muster confidence in it. In 301 he introduced his Edictum de Pretiis – a fixed income and wages policy to check inflation – an unsuccessful idea still attempted in our contemporary society. Despite harsh penalties it failed dismally with goods disappearing from the market.

OBVERSE: The bust of Constantine, in profile right, with draped cuirass and epaulettes, has a diadem fastened with orbicular tipped ties and is surrounded by the legend and a border of pellets.

306 – 337 AD
ROME
CONSTANTINE I,
THE GREAT
FLAVIUS VALERIUS
CONSTANTINUS,
Bronze Follis
3,53 grams
20 mm diameter
Struck at Treviri Mint

↑

CONSTANTINUS P[ ]F[ ]AUG[ ]

CONSTANTINE PIUS, BLESSED AUGUSTUS

REVERSE: Sol, the sun god, stands on a short exergual ground line. His crowned head is in profile left, he is semi-nude and his cloak draped over his left shoulder and upper arm flows behind. He holds a globe in his left palm and gesticulates with his right hand. He is flanked by the officinia marks TF and in the exergue the mintmark BTR. The coin is encircled by the legend and a border of pellets.

SOLI INVICTO COMITI   TF
                        BTR

TO THE SUN INVINCIBLE – HIS COMPANION

The Roman Empire became fragmented during the barbarian invasions when great hordes of Huns and Goths surged across Europe and the Mediterranean. Constantine, impressed by the strategic importance of Byzantium (from Byzas, the Greek mythological hero), founded Constantinople on its site as the new Rome, a separate Eastern Empire from 395 AD. Although Constantine accepted Christianity as early as 313 AD he remained a syncretist and harmonised Christianity and the cult of the sun. He was instrumental in steering Christians from a powerful though persecuted minority to effective supremacy. The Byzantine Empire, at its height, dominated the Balkan Peninsula, Asia Minor, Crete, Cyprus and Southern Italy and continued for over a thousand years, falling to the Mohammedan Turks in 1453 AD. Greek culture was kept alive in the Byzantine Empire during the dark ages and helped to kindle Western Renaissance.

see pages 159, 160

383 – 408 AD
CONSTANTINOPLE
ARCADIUS, FLAVIUS
Gold Solidus
4,48 grams
20 mm diameter
Struck at Sirmium
↓

see pages 161, 162

OBVERSE: The bust of Arcadius is draped with a paludamentum, a cloak worn by the Emperor, over a cuirass and fastened by a fibula, a brooch which has a roundel and triple pendant. He is flanked by the legend and is surrounded by an embossed patterned rim. The wistful, introspective expression of this young emperor is revealing. He was a weak and ineffectual ruler whose government was successively in the hands of his ministers.

OUR LORD ARCADIUS PIUS BLESSED AUGUSTUS

REVERSE: Uniformed Arcadius stands triumphant on a short exergual ground line, inclined right. He holds a standard in his right hand and the winged Victory on his outstretched palm is about to crown him with a laurel wreath. He subdues a cowering bearded captive – who looks somewhat downtrodden! Arcadius is flanked by the initials S M and the exergue bears the inscription COMOB. The coin is surrounded by a raised patterned border.

VICTORIA AVG[VSTORVM]

VICTORY OF THE TWO CAESARS

COM[ES AVRI] OB[RYZVM]

THE GOLD CURRENCY OFFICIAL ATTESTED PURE

S M

SIRMIUM MINT

100

OBVERSE: This delightful group is that of the Emperor Heraclius and his little son Heraclius Constantine. The Emperor's facing bust (foreground left) is draped in a chlamys, the long (purple) cloak assumed at the imperial coronation. It is fastened at the right shoulder with a jewel encrusted fibula, comprised of a loop with triple pendant surmounted by a roundel. He wears a jewelled crown with cruciform crest and has a beard and moustache. The bust of his infant son, facing, is similarly draped and bedecked with a fibula and cruciform crested coronet. In the field is the Holy Cross symbol and from the left is a semi-circular inscription. The coin is struck on a large flan and shows traces of a patterned border at its base.

OUR TWO LORDS* HERACLIUS AND HERACLIUS CONSTANTINE, FATHERS OF THE FATHERLAND

REVERSE: A cross potent stands on a base and three degrees, surrounded by the legend, and shows traces of a patterned border above.

AUGUSTAN VICTORY

GOLD CURRENCY OFFICIAL ATTESTED PURE

Byzantine coins have distinctive embossed lines, pellets and Christian symbols. Heraclius ruled in turbulent and eventful times. In 614 AD the Persians took Jerusalem and Damascus and carried off the Holy Cross. In 625 AD Heraclius repelled an attack on Constantinople by the Avars and Persians and decisively defeated them at Nineveh. In 628 AD he won back

610–641 AD
CONSTANTINOPLE
HERACLIUS AND
HERACLIUS
CONSTANTINE
Gold Solidus
4,60 grams
21 mm diameter
Minted at
Constantinople
613–616 AD
↓

see page 171

*Dominus Noster = dn   Our two Lords = dd nn

the Holy Cross, only to be defeated later by Omar I, 2nd Kaliph, Mohammed's advisor in a Holy War.

978 – 1016 AD
ENGLAND
Late Anglo Saxon
AETHELRED II,
The Unready
Silver Long Cross Penny
1,67 grams
19 mm diameter
Minted at Liher
(Leicester)
Moneyer – Aelfric
Initial mark:
Symbol of Christ
↗

see page 172

OBVERSE: The bust of Aethelred, in profile left, has a drape fastened in the front by an oval clasp and there is an oval shaped pellet in the field behind his neck. He is surrounded by the legend and a pearled border. This remarkable bust, though of relatively primitive execution, is ablaze with vitality. It has been enhanced by time and is toned with turquoise, purple and gold hues – a superb specimen.

✠ÆÐELRED REX ANGLO[RVM]

AETHELRED, KING OF THE ENGLISH

REVERSE: The Long Cross is voided and its limbs terminate in triple crescents. It is surrounded by the legend and a pearled border.

✠ÆLFRIC MO[NETA] LIHER

AELFRIC (THE MONEYER) LEICESTER MINT

During the reign of Aethelred II England was subjected to successive Viking raids.

This specimen is typical of the coin used as Danegeld – a national tax paid by the English to maintain a force to oppose the Danes, or to procure peace. It later became a tax levied by the Danish princes on every hide of land owned by the Anglo Saxons. Minting activity was profuse during this period in England, with some seventy-five different mints and a host of moneyers. These English coins are said to be found in greater quantity in Denmark than in England.

OBVERSE: The bust of Christ facing is invested with a tunic and himation (rectangular drape worn as a cloak) and has a beard, moustache and long hair with a centre parting. He is adorned by a nimbus with a voided cross potent which has a small crescent in its upper quarters, an emblem of Byzantium which symbolises the Virgin Mary as Queen of Heaven. His right hand is in a gesture of benediction as he clasps a closed book of the gospel in his left. The coin is surrounded by the legend and a concentric patterned border.

✠ IҺS [IҺϚOYϹ] XI Ϛ [X(P)I(ϚTO)Ϲ]
RЄX RЄGNANTIҺM
JESUS CHRIST, KING OF KINGS

1025 – 1028 AD
CONSTANTINOPLE
CONSTANTINE VIII
Gold Histamenon
4,39 grams
26 mm diameter
Minted at
Constantinople
Initial mark:
Symbol of Christ
↓

REVERSE: The facing bust of Emperor Constantine VIII is draped in a richly ornamented loros, a consular robe that became associated with the Emperor's religious authority. It symbolised the winding sheet of Christ and, by its embellishments, his resurrection. Originally draped according to complex ceremonial dictates, it later assumed this simplified form. His crown has a cruciform crest and prependovlia, hanging pieces, now generally referred to as pendilia – ornaments that were suspended from the crown over the ears. In his right hand he holds a labarum, previously a Roman military standard to which Constantine added the Chi-Rho symbol. This symbol is thought to be the first two Greek letters of Christ's name seen by Constantine in a vision and placed on his standard and the shields of his soldiers to place them under Christ's protection. In his left hand he holds an akakia, a purple silk bag centrally bound with a white cloth tie containing dust, a symbol of mortality. He is surrounded by a semi-circular legend punctuated by a cruciform initial mark and a pellet stop within concentric borders of denticles.

see pages 173, 174

continued

103

✠ CWNSTANTIN BASILEYS ROM[AION]

CONSTANTINE, KING OF THE ROMANS

Constantine VIII, Augustus since 962 AD, assumed full power on the death of his co-Emperor Basil II. His reign was brief and uneventful.

1028 – 1034 AD
CONSTANTINOPLE
ROMANUS III
Gold Histamenon
4,28 grams
24 mm diameter
Minted at
Constantinople
Initial Mark:
Symbol of Christ
↓

see pages 175, 176

OBVERSE: The facing figure of Christ has long hair with a centre parting, a beard and a moustache, and is enthroned on a broad, square-backed, upholstered seat which has a frame embellished with patterns of pellets. He wears a tunic and himation and has a voided cross nimbus behind His head. His right hand rests in the fold of His vestment, and His left hand supports a book of the gospel. His right leg is inclined to the left and His feet are bare. He is flanked by the legend and is surrounded by concentric patterned borders.

✠ IhS[uS OYC] XIS [X(P)I(STO)C] REX REGNANTIhM

JESUS CHRIST, KING OF KINGS

REVERSE: Romanus III, facing, stands to the left. He wears a loros, richly ornamented with pellets and geometric tracery, and a crown with cruciform crest and pendilia. His right hand is in a benign gesture and his left holds a globus cruciger, symbolic of the whole world and the Emperor's domination over it as the representative of Christ. Standing on the right is the habited Virgin Mary with nimbus, wearing a tunic and decorated maphorion (long veil). Her right hand touches his crown and Her left is in a gesture of blessing. Between their heads in the field is an akakia symbol and the letters MΘ(Mother of God). The group is flanked by the legend within concentric patterned borders.

OF THE ROMANS   MOTHER OF GOD

Romanus III was held in low esteem by the historian Psellus who, in his chronicles, roundly censured him for his ambitious pursuit of military honour and the inglorious Arab War that he is said to have instigated and in which he failed to emulate the exploits of Alexander the Great.

OBVERSE: The bust of Christ, facing, is draped in a tunic and himation. His long hair has a centre parting and He has a beard and moustache. Christ is adorned with a nimbus which has a voided cross and a small crescent in each of its upper quarters. His right hand is in a gesture of benediction and He clasps a closed book of the gospel, and is surrounded by the legend and concentric patterned borders of pellets, on the convex side of the planchet.

JESUS CHRIST, KING OF KINGS

REVERSE: The facing half-length figure of Constantine IX has a beard, moustache and wears a jewel encrusted cruciform crested crown with pendilia and a loros, magnificently embellished in a geometric design of pellets and tracery. He holds a cruciform sceptre in his right hand and a globus cruciger in his left. The legend is arched above and surrounded by concentric patterns of pellets within a triple border of pellets on the concave side of the planchet.

1042 – 1055 AD
CONSTANTINOPLE
CONSTANTINE IX
Gold Histamenon
scyphate –
cup shaped planchet
4,38 grams
28 mm diameter   ↓
Minted at
Constantinople
Initial Mark:
Symbol of Christ

105

✠ CWИSTAИTIИ BASILEYS ROM[AIAИ]

CONSTANTINE, KING OF THE ROMANS

see page 177 Constantine IX was a light-hearted man with a keen sense of humour. He was a patron of literature and restored the Constantinople University. However, according to Psellus, his reign was a disaster. Neglect of both government and army and the squandering of the treasury of Basil II are cited. His reign marked the beginning of the Empire's decline and the schism between the Eastern and Roman churches.

1157 – 1182 AD
DENMARK
KING VALDEMAR I,
THE GREAT
Silver Penning (Penny)
0,89 grams
17 mm diameter
Struck at Lund in Skaane
↓

OBVERSE: The facing bust is a symbolic portrayal of King Valdemar I. He is invested and crowned, and holds a sceptre in his right hand and a globus cruciger in his left, and is encircled by a border of pellets.

REVERSE: The facing bust is that of the Archbishop of Lund. He is draped in a vestment which has a large broad collar and centre panel decorated with pellets. He wears a crown with pendilia and in his right hand holds what appears to be a Yggdrasil, the tree of life, knowledge, time and space with branches symbolising heaven, earth and hell. In his left hand is an archiepiscopal staff and he is surrounded by a border of pellets.

The effigies are stylised representations with no apparent attempt at character portrayal. They rely on royal insignia and Christian symbols to identify the persons portrayed. These see page 178 quaint strikings are comprised of simple lines and pellets and with their ecclesiastical affiliations show Byzantine influence and a strong basic design.

Valdemar Knudsson, the victor of the War of the Princes,

fought for the Danish succession on the death of Eric III. After the battle of Grate Heath in 1157 he emerged as King of Denmark and his reign was a long and glorious one. He was openly opposed to the Hanseatic bid to control the important herring trade of the Baltic, delivered his country from the fury of the Wendish warriors, and worked in close collaboration with the church.

The Archbishop of Lund and the Bishop of Roskilde enjoyed minting rights. The coinage at that time reverted from the bracteates to the two-sided Penning which was of good silver but became badly debased.

Archbishop Eskil was opposed to the strength of the monarchy and on his final retirement in 1177 the King's close childhood friend, the powerful Bishop Absolom, was elevated to archbishop. His reluctance to accept the position was overcome by unusual Papal dispensation which allowed him to continue to control the See of Roskilde as well as that of Lund.

1201 – 1213 AD
GERMANY
JOHANN I,
The Benedictine Abbot
Silver Pfaffenpfennig
(Parson's Penny)
Approx 0,82 grams*
42 mm diameter
Minted at Hersfeld
Abbey

see page 179

OBVERSE: The Abbot Johann I, facing, stands in long vestment with diapered collar and holds a crosier in his left hand (symbolic shepherd's crook) and in the other an open book which symbolises the book of life and the wisdom of the scriptures. He is surrounded by the legend and concentric patterned borders of pellets and tracery.

𝕴𝕺𝕳𝕬𝕹𝕹𝕰𝕾 𝕳𝕰𝕽𝕾𝕱𝕰𝕷𝕯𝕰𝕹𝕾𝕴𝕾

JOHANNES HERSFELDENSIS   JOHANNES OF HERSFELD

REVERSE: As obverse in intaglio.
Pfaffenpfennige have been known as Bracteates from the eighteenth century onwards (Latin *bractea* – thin piece of metal). They are characteristically symbolic renderings relying on figures and religious symbols with little attempt at character portrayal.
The design of these quaint coins was embossed into a wafer-thin planchet struck with a single die into a pliable base, the resultant mirrored impression appearing in intaglio on the reverse. These fragile issues enjoyed wide circulation in Europe until the early part of the fourteenth century.

*Specimen has repair at 6 o'clock

OBVERSE: King Edward III, clad in armour and in a resolute posture, appears to be walking through the ornate Gothic porch which stands on pedestals strengthened by a plinth at the base of the portals. The pitched and pinnacled uprights are enriched with quatrefoil crested columns and spanned by an elaborate ogee arch, embellished with a fleuron finial and three crockets on either side. It is supported by a tressure of five arches and decorated with a pellet on each cusp. The armour-clad monarch wears a crowned basinet, a chain mail coat with a broad gorget, couteres and a jupon, greaves solle-rets and spurs. He shoulders a large sword with a tapered blade, a hilt with curved cross-piece and a large pommel. He holds a shield in his left hand which displays the new practice of quartering which he adopted in 1340 when he marshalled the Arms of France semé-de-lis. The shield is emblazoned quarterly: 1 & 4 Semé-de-lis (France); 2 & 3 Three lions-leopardé passant guardant per pale (England) as an expression of his claim to French sovereignty.

Beneath his feet are two lions-leopardé, recumbant guardant, with long meandering tails. There is a mintmark (La) R(ochelle) between the right hand pinnacles of the porch. The thin hammered flan is surrounded by the legend which is arranged circumferentially between the devices and protected by concentric borders of denticles.

1327 – 1355 AD
FRANCE, AQUITAINE
ANGLO – GALLIC
KING EDWARD III
Gold Guiennois
3,93 grams
30 mm diameter
Struck at the
La Rochelle Mint
Mintmark: R(ochelle)
Initial marks:
Obverse – Fleuron
(crest on the portico)
Reverse – Cross patée
←

EDWARD BY THE GRACE OF GOD, KING OF ENGLAND AND LORD OF AQUITAINE

REVERSE: The florid cross botonné has a central quatrefoil and tri-corporate limbs with trefoil terminals enriched with foliaged fleurons. There are fleurs-de-lis and lions-leopardé, passant reguardant, displayed quarterly between the limbs. The cross is surrounded by a tressure of sixteen arches each

see page 180

of their cusps decorated with a single pellet, and the legend within concentric denticular borders.

GLORY TO GOD ON HIGH AND PEACE ON EARTH

Edward III laid claim to the French throne and assumed the French royal title in 1337 and the Hundred Years War with France followed. He proved to be a successful monarch and was brave and chivalrous, albeit self-centred and merciless. He gained several French territories and as a statement of his right by conquest he issued a new coin – the Guiennois. The peace motto which appears on the reverse suggests his desire to normalize relations and Anglo-Gallic trade.

1328 – 1350 AD
FRANCE
KING PHILIP VI
(DE VALOIS)
Gold Écu d'or
4,50 grams
29 mm diameter

OBVERSE: The King is seated on an elaborate Gothic style throne which stands on a dais embellished with a floral motif. The broad seat shown in perspective has four elaborately pinnacled composite posts, fretwork and an engrailed edged backrest. The King's crown is a simple circlet heightened by four cusps each surmounted by a large fleur-de-lis and his long locks fall from beneath the crown on either side. King Philip wears a coat of mail, a tabard, greaves and sabatons. He shoulders a drawn sword on his right and his left hand supports a shield edged with pellets and charged with the French arms, semé-de-lis, originally borne by Louis VII of France (1137 – 1180). This charge was subsequently changed to three fleurs-de-lis in honour of the Holy Trinity. The seated monarch is framed by a tressure of eight arches echoed with tracery, embellished with a trefoil in each of the spandrels, within a denticular border. The coin is encircled by the legend which is arranged to accommodate the dais and is protected by a border of denticles.

* Spelling error on coin, should be EXCELSIS

110

✠ PHILIPPVS:DEI·GRA[   ]FRANCORVM:REX

PHILIP, KING OF THE FRENCH, BY THE GRACE OF GOD

First issue struck at the
La Rochelle Mint
circa 1337 AD
Initial mark: Cross patée
✓

REVERSE: The cross is elaborately structured with tri-corporate limbs, the outer sections of which are beaded, and there is a quatrefoil in the centre. The end of each limb is terminated in a quatrefoil from which spring three trefoils. The cross is within a quatrefoil boss, embellished with a beaded inner border, and a fleuron on each cusp. There is a trefoil in each of the spandrels and the coin is surrounded by the legend within a concentric denticular border.

see pages 181, 182

✠XP[   ]C[   ] :VINCIT XP[   ]C[   ] REGNAT
XP[   ]C[   ] IMPERAT*

CHRIST CONQUERS, CHRIST RULES, CHRIST COMMANDS
The legend is the war cry used by the first crusaders and occurs frequently on French regal issues.

The succession of Philip VI to the French throne was challenged by Edward III of England and the Hundred Years War ensued. Philip was defeated by Edward III and his country continued to be troubled by war and was beset, as was the rest of Europe, by the dreadful Black Death, a form of bubonic plague. Trade was disrupted and owing to the debasement of French coinage demands were made for payment in gold.

*Spelling errors on coin, should be REGNAT, IMPERAT

1355–1371 AD
FRANCE,
ANGLO-GALLIC
EDWARD OF
WOODSTOCK,
The Black Prince,
Ruler of Aquitaine
Gold Pavillon d'or
5,42 grams
32 mm diameter
Initial mark:
Cross potent
First issue struck at
Poitiers

↖

see pages 184, 185

OBVERSE: The Prince stands, facing, beneath a Gothic porch. He has long hair and wears a coronet which is a simple circlet heightened with roses. He is invested in a robe with long full sleeves, a square neckline, and a fur-lined mantle fastened across the chest with an ornamental chain. The fur is indicated by a vair pattern which appears vertically from below his left elbow. He shoulders a great sword on his right. The sword has a long broad blade which tapers acutely from the hilt and has a fuller (blood channel). The cross-piece is slightly curved and the two-handed grip has a large round pommel. The Prince points with the index finger of his left hand towards the sword in a triumphant gesture suggesting his right to sovereignty and his rule by force of arms. This is an intentional parody of the magnificent gold Pavillon of Philip VI (1328 – 1350) which portrays the French monarch enthroned beneath a pavilion shouldering a sceptre to which he points in a similar manner. The Black Prince is flanked by four stylised ostrich feathers, two on either side. Their tips are inclined to the right and their quills pass through escrolls. They are said to commemorate his having displumed the helm of John, King of Bohemia at the battle of Crecy in 1346*. At the Prince's feet are two lions-leopardé couchant guardant to the left and right respectively. The portal of the Gothic porch is pitched, pinnacled and enriched with crockets, annulets and tricorporate posts topped with foliated trefoil tracery. The intrados is braced with ornamental arches with a pellet on each cusp, the plate tracery is embellished with a quatrefoil, and there is a finial ornament on the ridge. The rafters support a balustrade enriched with annulets, quatrefoils, and an engrailed edge decorated with pellets. There is a tracery of arches with a pellet on each cusp, positioned radially to the left and right of the porch, as is the legend which is between concentric borders of denticles – a numismatic triumph in Gothic art.

*See footnote on page 114

EDWARD FIRST BORN OF THE KING OF ENGLAND PRINCE
OF AQUITAINE

REVERSE: This spectacular and original design presents an
elaborate juxtaposition of symbols and geometric patterns.
The acorn ended stalks, with foliage, spring from annulets to
form the limbs of a cross. In the centre is a faux lozenge with
curved facets and a central cinquefoil. In the angles are
fleurs-de-lis and rampant lions leopardé, saltirewise. These
devices are individually framed by the skilful positioning of
the oak leaves which are joined by stems of tracery. This
delightful cruciform composition is within an eight-pointed
star which is comprised of an octagonal lozenge with parallel
borders, superimposed on a similarly bordered square. The
points of the lozenge are decorated with arched tracery and a
trefoil on each cusp. In each angle of the square is a quatrefoil braced with tracery and there is a trefoil in each of the
eight spandrels. The design is completed by a circle and the
legend between concentric borders of denticles.

THE LORD IS MY STRENGTH AND MY SHIELD, MY HEART
HATH TRUSTED IN HIM – *Psalm XXVIII. 8*

The Black Prince was the eldest son of Edward III of
England. The chivalrous young Prince showed great aptitude
for hunting and the arts of war and as a youth of sixteen com-
manded a wing of his father's army at the battle of Crecy. He
arrived at Bordeaux as his lieutenant and led several successful campaigns and conquered considerable French territory.
He was declared Prince of Aquitaine by Royal Charter in

1362. His subjects were alienated by his harsh and inflexible intolerance and he ordered the merciless massacre of the rebellious people of Limoges in 1370. He received vast payments of gold coin from the French, after the battle of Bretigny, under the complex rules of ransom, and recoined this large spectacular issue which rivalled the magnificent French regal issues.

His health was ruined, in Spain, whilst he was aiding Pedro the Cruel to recover Castille in 1367 and finally, in 1371, he was forced to give up the government of Aquitaine due to failing health and returned to England where he died in 1376.

*The feathers, together with the motto *Ich Dien* (I serve) on their escrolls were adopted as his badge, and three were incorporated as a charge on his "shield for peace". The device was thus introduced into English Royal Heraldry and continues to be used as a device for the heir apparent, the Prince of Wales

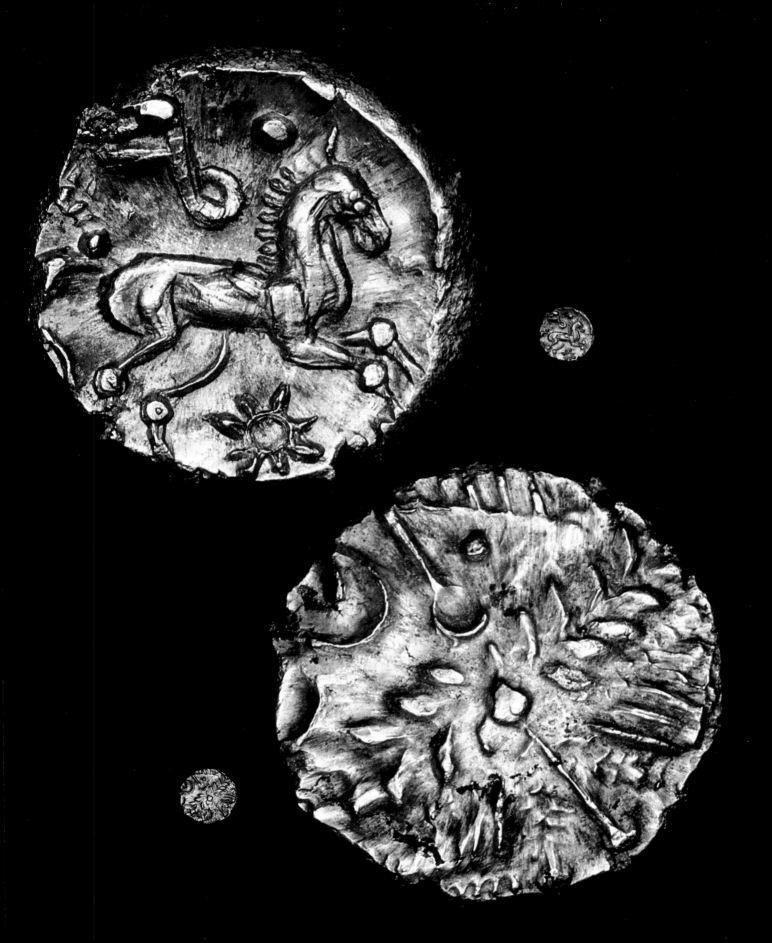

OBVERSE: Confronting full length figure of Sigismund who wears a coronet with a cruciform crest and a high dome, a suit of armour, cape and sword, and shoulders a sceptre. He is flanked by a lion holding the Austrian coat of arms left, its paws and semi-profile head to view. To the right is an armet with a panache surrounded by an engrailed border and the legend within concentric borders of denticles and finished with an embossed rim.

SIGISMVNDVS ARCHIDVX·AVSTRIA

SIGISMUND, ARCHDUKE OF AUSTRIA

REVERSE: The knight in full armour, his helmet with a panache, bears a standard and gallops on a charger right, its caparison flying in lively profusion. The date 1486 is positioned below the equestrian group which is encircled by fifteen shields surrounding a principal shield at the base. They are flanked by concentric borders of denticles and a raised rim. 1486

1439 – 1489 AD
AUSTRIA, TYROL
ARCHDUKE
SIGISMUND
Silver
Guldengroschen
31,54 grams
41 mm diameter
Minted in 1486 at
Hall near the rich
silver mines of Schwaz
Mintmark: Flower

Archduke Sigismund founded a mint at Hall and in 1484 struck the Guldengroschen, approximately the size of a Thaler, with the value of one gold Gulden. They gained wide acceptance and were soon copied when the demand for them increased, due to an acceleration of trade, principally a result of the activities of the silver mines in Tyrol and Bohemia and, from 1516, the famous mines of Joachimsthal.

see page 183

1469 – 1474 AD
FRANCE, AQUITAINE
CHARLES DE
FRANCE, DUKE OF
AQUITAINE,
BROTHER OF
LOUIS XI
Gold Hardi d'or
3,44 grams
27 mm diameter
Mintmark:
Obverse – Pheon flanked
by six pointed stars
(stops) at 12 o'clock and
a fleur-de-lis at 6 o'clock
Reverse – Pheon
↗

see page 186

OBVERSE: The facing three-quarter length effigy is that of the young Duke. He has long hair and wears a coronet with a circlet chased and heightened by fleurets and fleurs-de-lis. He is invested and wears a cape and bejewelled necklace and shoulders a great sword on his right. It has a long blade that tapers from the hilt, a fuller, two handed grip, crosspiece and a large pommel. He points to the war sword with the index finger of his left hand imitating the parody of the Black Prince's Pavillon d'or. The portrait is flanked by a tressure of arches decorated with a pellet on each cusp and surrounded by the legend within concentric borders of denticles. There are signs of clashed dies and traces of the reverse are visible.

A*KAROLVS *DVX* A*QVITANIE*

CHARLES, DUKE OF AQUITAINE

This splendent lifelike portrait is remarkable; its strong textures and energetic tracery suggest a style reminiscent of the impressionist painters of the nineteenth century.

REVERSE: The tri-corporate limbs and annulets of the elaborate cross potent have a solid framework flanked by thin supports. Each limb terminates in an acorn on a short stout stem from which spring oak leaves. The cross has a central quatrefoil and repeated saltirewise in the angles are fleurs-de-lis and lions leopardé. The cross is within a circular tracery embellished with bobbed cusps, and the legend within concentric borders of denticles.

XP[I]C[TOC] :VINCIT XP[I]C[TOC] REGNAT XP[I]C[TOC] IMPERAT

CHRIST CONQUERS, CHRIST RULES, CHRIST COMMANDS

The capricious young brother of King Louis XI of France hesitantly accepted the recreated Duchy of Aquitaine. How-

122

ever, he did not engender confidence as a ruler. The King was soon to hear rumours of his brother's requests to the Pope for dispensation to undo oaths made to him and of conspiracy against him which were circulating at the court of Aquitaine. The Duke died from disease at the age of twenty-five.

OBVERSE: The bust of Richard III facing, has scrolled locks, wears a crown and is encompassed by a double tressure of nine arches. Six of their cusps are enriched with fleurs-de-lis and encircled by a border of pellets and the legend.

RICHARD, BY THE GRACE OF GOD, KING OF ENGLAND AND FRANCE

REVERSE: A long cross patée with three pellets in each of its quartered sections is encompassed by concentric circles of pellets with the legend between them.

I HAVE MADE GOD MY HELPER   THE CITY OF LONDON

1483 – 1485 AD
ENGLAND
KING RICHARD III
Silver Groat, fourpence
8,85 grams
25 mm diameter
Initial mark:
Halved sun (six rays)
and rose
Struck at the Tower Mint
from dies by John Shaw
↑

Richard III, Duke of Gloucester, was the younger brother of Edward IV to whom he gave his loyal support during the latter stages of the Wars of the Roses. On the sudden death of his brother he became Protector of the Kingdom and the guardian of his young nephew Edward V, the little Duke of York, whom he confined to the Tower of London with his brother. The boys were never seen again and Richard assumed the crown.

see page 195

OBVERSE: Henry VII is seated majestically. His throne has a straight diapered back and is flanked on either side by ornate cruciform pillars. He wears an arched crown surmounted by an orb, has long hair, trailing vestments and a cape with ruffled collar, draw string and jewelled clasp. At his feet is a portcullis, the badge of the Beauforts and their descendants – the Tudor Sovereigns. In his left hand he holds an orb, and in his right hand a sceptre. His throne is decorated with fleurs-de-lis and pellets surrounded by a tracery within concentric borders of denticles which flank the legend.

HENRY, BY THE GRACE OF GOD, KING OF ENGLAND AND FRANCE, LORD OF IRELAND

REVERSE: The Tudor rose, introduced by Henry VII, is comprised of the united roses of the Houses of Lancaster (red) and York (white) and symbolises the unity between them after thirty years of war (Wars of the Roses). They are flamboyantly styled dog roses of five petals with a sepal between each petal of the larger bloom, embellished with stylised bunches of grapes and garniture, and centrally superimposed with the Royal Arms of England, emblazoned per cross with fleurs-de-lis and lions rampant. The legend is positioned circumferentially between borders of denticles.

BUT JESUS PASSING THROUGH THE MIDST OF THEM, WENT HIS WAY – *Luke IV. 30*

1485 – 1509 AD
ENGLAND
KING HENRY VII
Gold Sovereign,
twenty shillings
15,42 grams
42 mm diameter
Initial marks:
Obverse – Fleur-de-lis
Reverse – Crosslet and
pheon
Struck at the Tower Mint
1502 – 1509
↖

see pages 196, 197

Henry VII, a dour, level headed monarch, defeated Richard III at Bosworth Field thus ending the Wars of the Roses. He was the first of the Tudor Kings and laid a solid foundation to his royal line through his marriage to Elizabeth of York. With a well run administration he amassed a fortune, advanced the power and dignity of the crown and encouraged trade and exploration.

English coinage during his reign underwent radical change. In support of his diplomatic entrée into Europe and his peaceful overtures in many directions, he introduced a heavy gold issue in line with continental practice. Though the pound sterling had been used as a denomination for centuries, a pound coin (the Sovereign) had never been minted. The resultant issue, the largest English gold coin up to that time, was struck in 1489 and from the dormant medieval monotony flowered one of England's most magnificent coins, in all the splendour of Tudor Renaissance style. This is an original and exciting monument to sovereignty and imperial status.

OBVERSE: The young Queen stands facing in a ship, framed by furled sails and rigging, with sixteen cannons to view and flying her personal ensign, a fringed banner bearing her initial M. A crown is positioned above her loose flowing tresses and her dress has a straight neckline, wide sleeves and gathered full skirt, with jewelled girdle. She wears a pendant and a circular jewelled brooch. In her right hand she holds a drawn sword and her left hand supports a shield emblazoned with the Royal Arms of England. A full-blown rose floats on the waves amidships. The ship is surrounded by a pearled border and the legend is arranged circumferentially.

MARY BY THE GRACE OF GOD, QUEEN OF ENGLAND, FRANCE AND IRELAND 1553

1553 – 1554 AD
ENGLAND
QUEEN MARY –

Bloody Mary
Gold Ryal, fifteen
shillings
7,62 grams
36 mm diameter
Privy Mark:
Pomegranate
Struck at the Tower Mint
in 1553

REVERSE: A central full-blown rose, *en soleil* with sixteen rays, four of which form a floriated cross fleury. In each of the angles there is a lion passant guardant with crown above, all within a tressure of eight pearled arches echoed with tracery and the legend between concentric borders of pellets.

THIS IS THE LORD'S DOING AND IT IS MARVELLOUS IN OUR EYES – *Psalm CXVII. 23*

This great rarity, a superb example of Tudor Renaissance art is struck on a thin planchet in low relief.

see page 198 Mary was forcibly separated from her mother and made to conceal her Catholic beliefs at the court of her father Henry VIII who persecuted and humiliated her. She found happiness for a brief period married to Philip of Spain, later becoming an embittered and powerful monarch. Although she ascended the throne amid popular enthusiasm she was soon feared, hated and despised for persecuting and murdering a great number of Protestants, losing Calais to France and for her failure to deal with rising prices.

OBVERSE: Queen Elizabeth stands facing in a ship. She is splendidly attired in an elaborate quilted dress with a broad, bejewelled, square neckline, epaulettes, sleeves, and a lace breast coverchief and cuffs. A jewel encrusted centre panel terminating in a V shape extends below the waist of her tight fitting bodice and her skirt is flared from the hips. She wears a cartwheel shaped cambric ruff, its deep projecting frills stiffly starched and goffered with fan-shape fluting. Her wig is tightly coiffured and she wears a crown with a jewelled circlet heightened by pearl encrusted arches and a mound. Adorned with a pendant and rings, she holds a sceptre with a fleur-de-lis in her right hand and an orb in the left. Elizabeth dictated the fashions of her time. Her distinctive style of dress was elegant and extravagantly ornate but was constrictive, exaggerated and artificial; cosmetics and dyed wigs were worn at court. The Queen is framed by the masts, rigging, and furled sails of the ship. The stern and aftercabins are shown in perspective and there is a crow's nest on the mizzenmast above the lateen sail and a circular pulley on the fore-rigging. The hull is decorated longitudinally with a cross-bow motif and beneath fleurs-de-lis and lions leopardé with a geometric pattern below.

During this period English ships were decorated with the vivid contrasting colours of the Tudors.

A Tudor rose floats on the waves admidships and at the forecastle is a dolphin-striker (?) and the Queen's personal ensign, a fringed banner bearing the initial E. The coin is surrounded by a pearled border intersected by parts of the ship, accentuating the three dimensional aspect of the design. The legend, arranged circumferentially, terminates with a trefoil.

1558 – 1603 AD
ENGLAND
QUEEN ELIZABETH I,
Gold Ryal,
fifteen shillings
7,65 grams
35 mm diameter
Mintmark: Reverse–
Lombardic A
Fifth issue 1583 – 1585 at
the Tower Mint under
Sir Richard Martin,
warden and master
worker
↓

ELIZABETH: D : G : ANGLIAE : FRANCIAE : ET · HIBERNIAE : REGINA ·

ELIZABETH, BY THE GRACE OF GOD, QUEEN OF ENGLAND, FRANCE AND IRELAND

see page 207

REVERSE: A rose *en soleil* is surrounded by sixteen rays, four of which form a floriated cross fleury. In each of the angles there is a lion passant guardant with a crown above, all within a tressure of eight pearled arches echoed with tracery and a trefoil in each of the spandrels. The coin is surrounded by the legend between concentric borders of pellets.

IhS[IHeOnS]: ꝛVT[em]: TRꝛnSIEnS· Per· medIV[m]: ILLORVm·IBꝛT·ꝛ

BUT JESUS PASSING THROUGH THE MIDST OF THEM, WENT HIS WAY – *Luke IV. 30*

This remarkable specimen struck on a perfectly circular flan has an attractive red tone and is a numismatic triumph befitting the Elizabethan age.

OBVERSE: The crowned bust of Elizabeth, profile left, shows her peaked coiffure of tight curls flowing into loose falling tresses over the back of her ruff and the shoulders of her elaborate bejewelled dress. She is surrounded by the legend within concentric indented borders.

ELIZABETH·D[EI]:G·[RATIA] ANG·[LIAE] FRA·[NCIAE] ET·HIB·[ERNIAE] REGINA

ELIZABETH, BY THE GRACE OF GOD, QUEEN OF ENGLAND, FRANCE AND IRELAND

REVERSE: The shield within a cartouche, emblazoned with the Royal Arms is flanked by the letters ER and has a three dimensional crown above, all within concentric indented borders with the legend between.

1558 – 1603 AD
ENGLAND
QUEEN ELIZABETH I
Gold Pound,
twenty shillings
11,35 grams
38 mm diameter
Mintmark: Woolpack
This third issue was
struck at the Tower Mint
1594 – 1596 under the
direction of Sir Richard
Martin
↘

E R SCVTVM·FIDEI · PROTEGET·EAM·

THE SHIELD OF FAITH SHALL PROTECT HER

The crowns on both obverse and reverse appear to be in front of the inner borders, accentuating the three dimensional perspective of the coin which is a glorious statement of Elizabethan elegance.

Elizabeth, daughter of Henry VIII and Anne Boleyn, was a very popular Queen. In her youth, during the reigns of Edward VI and Mary I, she was suspected of treason and kept in semi-captivity. She was intelligent, well educated, strong-willed, brave and astute; qualities which aided her survival and endeared her to the nation. Upon her succession she inherited a divided country under threat from France and Spain. She remained unmarried and being a skilful diplomat the reasons were most probably political. She partially succeeded in satisfying the Protestants and Catholics and increased the power of England's navy. Her display of defiant

see page 208

137

courage in dealing with the Spanish Armada inspired and united her subjects and it was during this prosperous Elizabethan age that the arts, music, poetry and drama flourished in England.

1581 – 1602 AD
TRANSYLVANIA,
Northern Rumania
PRINCE SIGISMUND
BATHORI
Silver Thaler
27,96 grams
44 mm diameter
Mintmark: Cross patée
Struck at the
Klausenburg Mint in
1593

↑

see page 209

OBVERSE: The bust of the Prince is in semi-profile right. He has a moustache with upturned ends, stubbly beard, close cropped hair and a quiff to conceal his receding hairline. He wears an earring, a gorget round his neck, a ribbed cuirass, its breastplate accommodating his prominent paunch, floreated pauldrons (protecting his shoulders), and sleeves of mail, with couteres (at his elbows) and gauntlets. He shoulders a mace on his right and at his waist is a truncated hand in a gauntlet holding a partially drawn sword. He is flanked by the legend punctuated with floreated stops each with five petals and concentric borders of denticles.

SIGISMVNDVS ✺ BATHORI ✺

SIGISMUNDUS BATHORI

REVERSE: A crowned oval cartouche is emblazoned with the Royal Arms charged with three claws and held by angel supporters whose breasts protrude through their draped vestments which have round collars and wide sleeves. Below there are six pellets and an inverted fleur-de-lis. The coin is encircled by the legend which has floreated stops, within denticular borders. A central horizontal die crack is visible across the reverse planchet of this specimen.

✺ PRINCH*RS ✺ TRANSSYLVANIÆ ✺ 1593

PRINCE OF TRANSYLVANIA 1593

This splendid caricature is skilfully engraved and its three dimensional perspective is accentuated through the juxtaposition of bust and border.

* Spelling error on coin, should be PRINCIPS

138

OBVERSE: The crowned coat of arms of Holland is emblazoned with a rampant lion and flanked by the mark of value II (+) II (four Reales) and encircled by the legend and the date 1601 above, between concentric borders of pellets.

INSIGNIA · HOLLANDIÆ. 16 01

THE INSIGNIA OF HOLLAND 1601

REVERSE: A shield bearing the city arms of Amsterdam has three saltire crosses placed vertically on the pointed pale and is held by rampant guardant lion supporters. Above is a twin arched bejewelled crown which appears three dimensional, and the coin is surrounded by concentric patterned borders of lozenges, the legend within.

ET · CIVITATIS · AMSTELREDAMENSIS · ❀

AND THE CITY OF AMSTERDAM

1601 AD
THE NETHERLANDS,
HOLLAND
Issued by The United
Amsterdam Company
Silver Half Daalder,
Four Reales
13,55 grams
33 mm diameter
Initial mark:
Flower of five petals
Minted at Dordrecht
under the direction of the
mintmaster Jacob Jansz
de Jonge

The Dutch were persecuted by Philip of Spain for their Protestant beliefs and in 1579 the seven northern provinces were united by William of Nassau, Prince of Orange (William the Silent), to form a Republic, and they were engaged in a succession of bloody campaigns – the Eighty Years War from 1568-1648. The seventeenth century heralded the golden age of Dutch sea power, when their commerce and exploration covered the globe and brought great prosperity. This trading issue was struck in competition to the Spanish Eight Reales (Pieces of Eight)* which enjoyed a wide circulation. In 1601 an articulated series of eight, four, two, one, half and quarter Reales were struck in small numbers. The various companies for distant trade amalgamated the following year and on March 20th, 1602, The Vereenigde Oostindische Compagnie – The United East India Company – was incorporated.

see page 210

*See page 187

OBVERSE: The facade of the city of Hamburg has corniced and embattled stone walls, an arched gateway, barred with a portcullis and surmounted by a barbican, flanked by castled towers, with conical roofs each with an orb. The date 1620 appears between the towers in the field and the coin is encircled by the legend which is underlined within a denticular border.

THE NEW COINAGE OF THE CITY OF HAMBURG 1620

REVERSE: The twin headed imperial eagle, its wings elevated and displayed, has its nimbate heads in profile to the left and right respectively. On its breast is an orb inscribed with the mark of value 32 (thirty-two schillings) which appears to form the support for a Latin cross which has a crown above. The coin is encircled by the legend within a concentric border of denticles.

FERDINANDUS· II:D[EI] :G[RATIA] :ROMA[NORUM] :IMP[ERATOR] :SE[MPER] :AU[GUSTUS] ㉜

FERDINAND II, BY THE GRACE OF GOD, EMPEROR OF THE ROMANS, EVER AUGUST

This twin headed eagle was adopted as the emblem of the Holy Roman Empire and symbolised its dominion over both the Eastern and Western empires.

1619 – 1637 AD
GERMANY, HAMBURG
EMPEROR
FERDINAND II
Silver Thaler
28,58 grams
41 mm diameter
Initial mark:
Moorish head
←

see page 211

OBVERSE: King James stands facing in a ship flanked by masts and framed by its convergent rigging. There are eleven cannons to view and his ensign is emblazoned with his initial I. A Tudor rose floats on the waves amidships. He is crowned, has a dapper beard, walrus moustache and wears a cuirass, ornate pauldrons, vambraces and couters, and a tasselled collar. He has a drawn sword in his right hand, in his left he holds a large shield incorporating the new emblazonry: 1 & 4 Grand Quarters (France modern and England quarterly); 2 The Scottish rampant lion; 3 The Irish harp. The ship is encircled by the legend and concentric borders of denticles.

✳IACOBVS DE[I]:G[RATIA]:MA[GNAE] BRI[TANNIAE] :FR[ANCIAE]:ET:HIBERNIAE:REX·

JAMES, BY THE GRACE OF GOD, KING OF GREAT BRITAIN, FRANCE AND IRELAND

"Four things our Noble showeth unto me –
King, ship, and sword and power of the sea"
This couplet was inspired by the "King in Ship" design originally introduced during the reign of Edward III.

REVERSE: The central Tudor rose is surrounded by a *spur rowel*. The white rose *en soleil*, a badge of the House of York, was introduced as a coin device during the reign of Edward IV and was used up to and including the reign of James I. It was probably during his reign that it began to be referred to as a *spur rowel*, although the device had not been changed except for the rose which was altered to a Tudor rose. Four of the rays or spurs form the limbs of a floriated cross fleury and in the angles there are lions passant guardant with crowns above, all within an eight-arched tressure of pellets echoed with tracery and triple pellets in the spandrels. The coin is surrounded by the legend within concentric borders of denticles.

1603 – 1625 AD
GREAT BRITAIN
KING JAMES I
Gold Spur Ryal,
fifteen shillings
16,89 grams
33 mm diameter
Initial mark:
Escallop
Second coinage struck
in 1607
↓

see page 212

✠·A· D[OMI]NO: FACTVM ·EST· ISTVD ·ET· EST ·MIRABILE·

THIS IS THE LORD'S DOING AND IT IS MARVELLOUS

James, son of Mary Queen of Scots, ascended the Scottish throne in 1566. He gained the approval of his cousin Elizabeth I who appointed him as her successor. He was unpopular, conceited and tactless, and his belief in the Divine Right of Kings affronted parliament. In 1605 Guy Fawkes tried to blow up the Houses of Parliament in order to assassinate him and his ministers. James dealt harshly with the puritans and it was during his reign that the Pilgrim Fathers set sail for America.

1603 – 1625 AD
GREAT BRITAIN
KING JAMES I
Gold Rose Ryal,
thirty shillings and
from 1612 onwards
thirty-three shillings.

OBVERSE: The crowned King is seated majestically on a splendid throne which has a fringed canopy surmounted by scrolled ornature, a square back enriched with a motif of flowers and pellets, fluted legs and scrolled arms. In the field there is a diapered pattern of pellets decorated with fleurs-de-lis and Tudor roses. James, with dapper beard and moustache, is dressed in a long flowing vestment tied with a girdle, an ermine cape, adorned with a jewelled collar of quatrefoil links and pendant, a ruff, hose and pointed shoes with floral pompons. He holds a sceptre with fleur-de-lis head and with his other hand supports an orb on his left knee. The throne is flanked by a border of pellets and the legend, and at the base beneath his feet is a portcullis with chains – a remarkable portrait.

✠·IACOBVS·D:[EI] G:[RATIA] MAG:[NAE] BRIT:[ANNIAE] FRAN:[CIAE] ET HIB:[ERNIAE] REX·

JAMES, BY THE GRACE OF GOD, KING OF GREAT BRITAIN, FRANCE AND IRELAND

REVERSE: The shield is quartered by a cross, which extends

beyond it terminating in fleurons, emblazoned with the Royal Arms and bearing the mark of value XXX above. It is encircled by fleurs-de-lis, lions rampant and Tudor roses which form a surrounding pattern within concentric circles of pellets and the legend.

✳A D[OMI]NO: FACTVM EST ISTVD ET EST MIRAB[ILE]: IN OC[VLIS]: N[OST]RIS.

THIS IS THE LORD'S DOING AND IT IS MARVELLOUS IN OUR EYES – *Psalm CXVIII. 23*

12,48 grams
38 mm diameter
Initial mark: Spur rowel
Struck at the Tower Mint
1619 – 1620
↑

see page 213

OBVERSE: King Louis XIII, facing to the right, has prominent features and a promontoried truncation. His long, luxuriant locks fall behind and at the sides of his protruberant neck. He wears a laurel wreath with nine leaves to view and has a moustache with upturned waxed ends. The effigy is flanked by the legend, with the date 1641 below, and the coin is surrounded by an invected border.

1610 – 1643 AD
FRANCE
KING LOUIS XIII,
The Just
Gold demi Louis d'or
3,41 grams
20 mm diameter
Mintmark: A
Struck at the Paris mint
in 1641 from dies by
Jean Varin of Liège
↓

LVD[OVICVS]·XIII·D[EI]·G[RATIA] FR[ANCIAE] ·ET·NAV[ARRAE]· REX ·1641·

LOUIS XIII BY THE GRACE OF GOD, KING OF FRANCE AND NAVARRE 1641

REVERSE: The cruciform arrangement is comprised of the monogram of L(ouis) in four pairs, back to back, forming a central square. There is a double arched crown above each limb embellished with fleurs-de-lis and a floriated mound. In each angle of the cross is a fleur-de-lis and in the centre a circle and the Paris mintmark A. The motto is positioned radially between the crowns, punctuated with pellet stops and protected by an indented border.

see page 214

WITH CHRIST HE CONQUERS, REIGNS, COMMANDS

This issue, struck in high relief and fine style, marks a significant milestone in French monetary reform. Coinage in France, as elsewhere, was subject to widespread clipping and other fraudulent practices and eventually in 1640 the Paris mint adopted the idea of the mill press and produced a new articulated issue. The smallest gold coin of the issue, the demi Louis, was the same weight as the old Ecu d'or but was reduced to twenty-two carats — as a result the undervalued Ecu d'or of twenty-three carats soon disappeared from circulation.

King Louis XIII was sickly and of a pensive disposition, and had a violent relationship with his mother Marie de Medici. Whilst he presided as absolute monarch he found pressures of state tiresome and preferred to pursue other pleasures. The effective power behind his administration was that of Cardinal Richelieu.

OBVERSE: The crowned, half-length bust of the King, head in profile left, shows his hair in a profusion of luxuriant locks which cascade on to the breast plate of his ornate armour. He has a goatee and radiate moustache and his attire is completed with a sash draped from the epaulette on his right shoulder, embellished with a pendant and lace collar. Charles, who wears vambraces, holds a drawn sword with a butterfly cross piece, long fuller and a round pommel in his right hand and an olive branch in his left. In the field to the right is an Oxford plume. The King is surrounded by an inner pattern of ingots and the legend within a denticular border.

CAROLVS·D[EI]:G[RATIA]:MAG[NAE]:BRI[TANNIAE]: FRANCIAE]: ET. HIBER[NIAE]:REX·

CHARLES, BY THE GRACE OF GOD, KING OF GREAT BRITAIN, FRANCE AND IRELAND

REVERSE: The long banner unfurls circumferentially bearing the legend and terminates in three horizontal undulating scrolls which bear the "Declaration". Above, between the scrolls, is the mark of value III, repeated by three Oxford plumes; below, between the scrolls, is the date 1644 and Oxon (Oxford) beneath, all within a border of denticles.

EXVRGAT·DEVS·[ET] DISSIPENTVR· INIMICI[EIVS]

LET GOD ARISE AND LET HIS ENEMIES BE SCATTERED
Psalm LXVIII. 1

·RELIG[IO]:PROT[ESTANTIVM]:LEG[ES]:ANG[LIAE]: LIBER[TAS]PAR[LIAMENTI]:* III·1644·oxon·

THE RELIGION OF THE PROTESTANTS, THE LAWS OF ENGLAND, THE LIBERTY OF PARLIAMENT 1644

1625 – 1649 AD
GREAT BRITAIN
KING CHARLES I
Gold Triple Unite, sixty shillings small module
27 grams
42 mm diameter
Struck at Oxford in 1644
Obverse mintmark and initial mark:
Oxford plume
Reverse initial mark:
Five pellets

→

see page 215

*This declaration was made by Charles I to the Privy Council at Wellington on September 19th 1642

One of the finest specimens known, this spectacular issue is the largest denomination in the English hammered series. The skilful juxtaposition of the effigy and the inner border succeeds in producing a three-dimensional effect despite the low relief of this handsome, dignified portrait.

Charles I, advocate of the Divine Right of Kings, attempted to suppress successive parliaments and the resultant civil war between the King and his aggrieved parliamentarians, led by Oliver Cromwell, ended with his imprisonment and execution. After the King's final break with parliament, coins continued to be struck in London till his trial and execution which he faced with the admirable dignity of a royal martyr. Coins were also minted during the Civil War in some of the provincial towns in order to ensure continuity of supply to areas under Royallist control or siege, during which time college plate was melted down to meet the shortage of silver for coinage.

From a numismatic and artistic point of view this is one of the most interesting periods of the English series.

OBVERSE: The shield is charged with a diapered fimbriated cross of St. George which is wreathed with palm and laurel and surrounded by the legend and a border of pellets.*

THE COMMONWEALTH OF ENGLAND

REVERSE: The conjoined shields are those of England (St. George) and Ireland (St. Patrick) with the Irish harp which has an ornate frame with a semi-nude winged female figure. The mark value .XX. is centrally positioned above and the coin is encircled by the legend within concentric borders of pellets.

*The enlargement of the reverse of this particular specimen reveals evidence to suggest that the trussel (possibly the trial-die) was re-engraved

The coin is remarkable because it is the only issue in English coinage to bear an inscription entirely in English. The scope of its design was greatly restricted by the austere puritanical dictates of the regime, but the coin is not lacking in elegance. It suffered the satirical wit of the Royallists, who quipped, "God and the Commonwealth are on different sides." Imagination ran riot, because the tops of the conjoined shields were said to resemble buttocks and the coin was bawdily referred to as breeches money, "a fit stamp for the coin of the rump".

Cromwell, an ardent puritan, helped parliament secure East Anglia during the civil war. With no previous military experience he mustered a disciplined force, devoted to him, the Bible and the cause of parliament, and with Fairfax brought the war to an end. Cromwell was convinced that God's Will required the execution of Charles I and signed his death warrant.

His Irish campaign of fanatical and merciless cruelty against Roman Catholicism tarnished his reputation. He destroyed Charles II's alliance with the Scots by his victories at Dunbar and Worcester and emerged the most powerful man in England as Lord Protector. His patience lost with parliamentary corruption, he replaced it with an assembly known as the Bare Bones Parliament which proved unsuccessful. After quarrelling with his first parliament he ruled the country under eleven major generals. This soon proved unpopular and he formed a second parliament which offered him the crown. He declined though he was in effect king. He ruled by force and tyranny and, failing to establish a lasting system of government, died dispirited in 1658.

1649 – 1660 AD
ENGLAND
OLIVER CROMWELL,
Lord Protector
Gold Unite,
twenty shillings
9,00 grams
35 mm diameter
Mintmark: Sun, with face
Struck at the Tower mint
in 1649 from dies thought
to be the work of
John East, one of
Thomas Simon's
assistant engravers
↓

see pages 216, 217

OBVERSE: The laureate head of Oliver Cromwell, profile left, has a moustache and a tuft of hair below his bottom lip and is surrounded by the legend, a denticular border and a milled edge.

OLIVAR·D[EI]·GRATIA·RE[I]P[UBLICÆ]·ANG[LIÆ]·SCO[TIÆ]·ET·HIB[ERNIÆ]·&·PRO[TECTOR]

OLIVER, BY THE GRACE OF GOD, PROTECTOR OF THE COMMONWEALTH (OR REPUBLIC) OF ENGLAND, SCOTLAND AND IRELAND

1649 – 1660 AD
ENGLAND
OLIVER CROMWELL,
Lord Protector
Gold Pattern Broad,
twenty shillings
9,10 grams
29 mm diameter
Struck at Drury House,
London in 1656
→

see page 218

REVERSE: Crowned shield of the Commonwealth bearing quarterly: 1 & 4 The cross of St. George; 2 The saltire of St. Andrew; 3 The harp of Ireland with nine strings, St. Patrick. The inescutcheon bears the arms of Oliver Cromwell, a rampant lion. The coin is surrounded by the legend, denticular border and a milled edge.

·I 6 5 6·PAX·QVÆRITVR·BELLO

1656 PEACE IS SOUGHT BY WAR

This masterpiece is the work of the celebrated die engraver, Thomas Simon, and is complemented by the technical skill of the French mint engineer, Pierre Blondeau, who was responsible for its striking on his newly invented mill and screw press. Cromwell's lifelike portrait is charged with vitality: his deep-set piercing eyes and sculptured face are finished to the last minute detail, including the veins at his temple and on his neck. The dies are finished in frosted mezzotint, a technique whereby a die or portion thereof is frosted with uniform roughness. Apparent highlights and shadows are produced by partially smoothing small areas of the frosting. The portrait is finished with an undulating truncation on a mirrored field.

see page 219

These hubs, master dies cut in relief, were used to produce several incuse working dies bearing the principal device only. Supplementary devices, symbols, dates, etc., were then added with a hand punch so that alterations could be made and worn dies replaced without having to discard the painstaking and costly engraving of the original master dies.

OBVERSE: The facing invested bust is that of Martin Luther; at its base is an elaborate cartouche inscribed with the date 1661. The coin is encircled by the legend between plain concentric borders.

✠ Mart[in] · Luther der · H[eiligen] · Schrifft · D[oktor]: weiland pred[iger] : u[nd] : proff[esor] : z[zu] : wittenb[erg] : · 1661·

MARTIN LUTHER, DOCTOR OF THEOLOGY, FORMERLY PREDICANT AND PROFESSOR AT WITTENBERG 1661

REVERSE: The city view of Eisleben shows a windmill on a hill to the left, three birds and clouds in the sky above. Along the exergual groundline is a row of trees and in the exergue is a cartouche bearing a shield charged with the arms of the Count of Mansfeld. The coin is encircled by the legend which is within a rope patterned inner border and a wreath.

✠ G[g]ottes wort u[nd] Luthers Lehr v[v]erzehrt num · u[nd] ·nimmer mehr. [i]lebie

GOD'S WORD AND THE TEACHINGS OF LUTHER VANISHES NEITHER NOW OR EVER

1632 – 1666 AD
GERMANY, EISLEBEN
CHRISTIAN
FRIEDRICH,
The Count of Mansfeld
Silver three-quarter
Schautaler
21,71 grams
46 mm diameter
Initial mark: Clover
This Schautaler was struck in 1661 to commemorate the centenary of the Convention of Evangelical Princes in Naumburg in 1561

The principal revenue of Mansfeld, a small state in the region of the Harz silver mines, was derived from the prolific minting of silver coins. This centenary issue, struck after the Thirty Years War that ensued between the Protestants and the Catholics, commemorates the Confession of Augsburg of 1530 signed by the Protestant princes who formed the Shmalkaldic League against the Emperor Charles V and his Catholic allies.

Martin Luther (1483 – 1546) was born in Saxony of humble birth. He proved to have great academic ability and took a university degree before becoming an Augustan monk. On visiting Rome he was horrified at the opulence and grandeur of the Catholic Church which he saw as a sink of corruption.

He took particular exception to the sale of indulgences, a method of fund-raising whereby a sinner could purchase a passport to salvation and summary forgiveness for his transgressions without having to do penance. In 1517 an itinerant Dominican monk, John Tetzel, came to Germany to sell indulgences in order to raise money for the rebuilding of St. Peter's in Rome. Luther, incensed by his presence and mission, openly reproached and condemned him, and was prompted to compose and nail to the church door at Wittenberg the famous ninety-five theses in which he censured the Catholic Church and its sale of indulgences.

see page 220

The following year Luther was summoned to Augsburg to recant. His refusal incited the public burning of his books in Cologne and resulted in his excommunication and being branded a heretic. Luther retaliated by burning the Papal Proclamation (Bull) and the Cannon Law. His dissent against the Church and his popular support in Germany were of great concern to the Catholics, whose solid foundations had suffered the spirit of the Renaissance and had begun to show signs of cracking. Charles V summoned Luther to appear before the Diet of Worms promising him safe conduct. He appeared before this assembly but remained resolute and, consequently, was declared an outlaw in the Holy Roman Empire.

He set out for home but was "kidnapped" en route and taken to the Wartburg Castle by Duke Frederick the Wise, an ardent supporter who ensured his safe return and ultimately arranged a post for Luther at Wittenberg University where he translated the Bible into German. Aided by fiery sermons and the power of the printed word, his view that the gospel was the only true source of religious teaching, and that salvation was only won through the love of God, gained wide acceptance.

Luther won the support of several German princes whose claims to sovereignty over the Holy Roman Empire enjoyed his reciprocation, even during their cruel suppression of the peasant revolt against serfdom in 1524/5 when the peasants rallied under the banner of his teachings. In 1525 he married a nun, Catherine von Bora, who had left her convent under the influence of his teachings. Savage fighting ensued between Protestants and Catholics culminating in a compromise treaty signed at Augsburg in 1555 which gave each ruler religious dominion. However, the devastating Thirty Years War (1618 – 1648) claimed millions of lives and Germany was left fragmented.

1657 – 1705 AD
AUSTRIA, TYROL
EMPEROR LEOPOLD I,
The Hogmouth
Silver Doppelthaler
57,05 grams
47 mm diameter
Struck at Hall 1686 – 1696
Die engraver: Johann
Anton König
see page 221

OBVERSE: The laureate bust of Leopold I faces right. He wears a luxuriant periwig and a moustache, high triangular collar, pendant and ornate jewelled pauldrons and a cuirass. His portrait is wreathed and encircled by the legend within a denticular border. Leopold is portrayed in grand caricature with no apparent attempt to conceal his grotesque mouth and lower lip – a hereditary deformity which occurred in the Hapsburg family.

LEOPOLD BY THE GRACE OF GOD, ROMAN EMPEROR, EVER AUGUST, KING OF GERMANY, HUNGARY AND BOHEMIA

REVERSE: The displayed Austrian eagle with a laurel nimbus has its crowned squawking head in profile left and is encompassed by a wreath, the legend and a denticular border.

ARCHDUKE OF AUSTRIA, DUKE OF BURGUNDY, COUNT OF THE TYROL

OBVERSE: The draped laureate bust of King Charles II, profile right, has a pencil moustache, long luxuriant curls and a small Tudor rose below the truncation which denotes that the silver for the coin was mined in the west of England. The bust is flanked by the legend and surrounded by denticular milling.

CAROLVS · II·DEI GRA[TIA] ❀

CHARLES II BY THE GRACE OF GOD

REVERSE: The crowned shields are in a cruciform arrangement and are charged with the arms of England, Scotland and Ireland with the monogram CC in each of the angles and the Most Noble Order of the Garter in the centre. The legend appears between the crowns of the shields and is encircled by denticular milling.

REX· MAG[NAE] BR[ITANNIAE] FRA[NCIAE] ET· HIB[ERNIAE]·16 62

KING OF GREAT BRITAIN, FRANCE AND IRELAND 1662

After his father's execution Charles assumed the role of King in January 1649 and in February was proclaimed King of Scotland in Edinburgh. He came over to Scotland in 1650 and was crowned at Scone in January, 1651. After a series of adventures he escaped to France and lived in Europe for nine years. He returned to England to a tumultuous welcome from a nation which was weary of Cromwell's military despotism and he was crowned in 1661. Charles made up for his penniless exile with the pursuit of pleasure but was an able politician, a patron of science, navigation and architecture.

This remarkable specimen is superbly engraved and struck save for a few adjustment marks on the hair and wreath. It has deep, lustrous hues of purple and azure, tinged with pink and gold, a result of toning over centuries.

1660 – 1685 AD
GREAT BRITAIN
KING CHARLES II
Silver Pattern Crown
32,79 grams
39 mm diameter
First bust, rose below
with plain edge
Struck at the Tower Mint
in 1662 by Pierre
Blondeau from dies by
the Roettier brothers
↓

see page 223

The success of Blondeau's milling technique can be appreciated by comparing this specimen with the enlargement of the gold Unite on page 222 which is described on page 166.

THE PETITION CROWN

The King was very dissatisfied with the current issue of his coins and wished to have fresh designs prepared. Thomas Simon, Chief Engraver at the mint, should have engraved the dies for the new coin issue but it was not to be. Charles, while in exile, had become acquainted with the Roettier family of goldsmiths and medallists in Antwerp, who, it is said, advanced money to him in return for his promise that he would find positions for the Roettier sons at the Tower Mint should he be returned to the throne. He was true to his word and in 1662 ordered Thomas Simon and Jan Roettier each to submit a trial piece for his new coinage. This resulted in a clash of artistic temperament and professional jealousy. Simon procrastinated and the impatient and possibly biased King accepted Jan Roettier's pattern. Though resolute in his decision, in 1663 the King ordered Roettier to improve his dies. Simon seized the opportunity of this belated dissatisfaction and presented the King with his famous "Petition Crown", a masterpiece in elegant baroque style, which like Roettier's was inspired by a likeness of the King by his limner, Samuel Cooper. Below the truncation of the bust is the signature, Simon, and on the edge the famous double row petition: *"THOMAS SIMON most humbly prays your MAJESTY to compare this his tryall piece with the Dutch and if more truly drawn & emboss'd more gracefully order'd and more accurately engraven to relieve him."*
Although it was superior, Simon's trial piece was rejected; he remained at the Tower Mint but was never reinstated as chief engraver. Simon was succeeded by Thomas Rawlins, who was instated as Chief Engraver in 1660. Roettier was appointed "one of the Chief Engravers of the Mint" in 1662 and Chief Engraver in 1670.

THOMAS SIMON · MOST · HVMBLY · PRAYS · YOVR · MAJESTY · TO · COMPARE · THIS · HIS · TRYALL · PIECE · WITH · THE · DVTCH · AND · IF · MORE
TRVLY · DRAWN · & · EMBOSS'D · MORE · GRACE: MAJESTY · FVLLY · ORDER'D · AND · MORE · ACCVRATELY · INGRAVEN · TO · RELIEVE · HIM.

XXXV

A most curious Crown-piece made by Tho. SIMON.

The Great Seal for the Order of the GARTER. T.S.

*The Ingenious Artists,
Brothers,
Abraham SIMON
& Thomas SIMON.
An°. 1663.*

A. SIMON.

T. SIMON.

G. Vertue fc. 1751.

165

1660 – 1685 AD
GREAT BRITAIN
KING CHARLES II
Gold Unite
9,00 grams
32 mm diameter
Initial mark: Crown
Second issue struck 1660 – 1662 at the Tower Mint from dies by Thomas Simon
↙

see page 222

OBVERSE: The laureate bust of King Charles II with a neat waxed moustache, profile left, is adorned with a profusion of luxuriant coiffured curls which cascade over his shoulders. The breastplate has a central motif comprised of a semi-circular sun of twelve rays surmounted by a facing head. There is a mark of value to the right in the field XX and the coin is encircled by the legend, within a denticular border.

CAROLVS·II·D[EI]·G[RATIA]·MAG[NAE]·BRIT[ANNIAE]
·FRAN[CIAE]·ET·HIB[ERNIAE]·REX ♔ XX

CHARLES II, BY THE GRACE OF GOD, KING OF GREAT BRITAIN, FRANCE AND IRELAND

REVERSE: The oval cartouche charged with the Royal Arms is crowned, flanked by the initials CR, and encircled by the legend within a denticular border. The superiority of the machine inevitably triumphed over the hammered technique and this is the final issue of the beautiful English hammered series and also the last English coin to bear a mintmark.

·FLORENT·CONCORDIA·REGNA· CR

THROUGH CONCORD KINGDOMS FLOURISH

OBVERSE: The pine tree with serrated patterned roots and branches is encircled by the legend, punctuated with patterns of pellets, within concentric borders of denticles.

IN ⁙ MASATHVSETS ⁙

IN MASSACHUSETTS

REVERSE: The date 1652 and the mark of value XII beneath are encircled by the legend within concentric borders of denticles.

NEW ENGLAND · AN[NO] · DO[MINI] 1652 XII

NEW ENGLAND ANNO DOMINI 1652 – XII

1652 – 1682 AD
AMERICA,
MASSACHUSETTS
COLONY
Silver Pine Tree Shilling
4,51 grams
24 mm diameter
Struck in Boston by
John Hull from 1652
↑

The early settlers of New England did not have their own currency and resorted to barter and bookkeeping. However, the surge in trade and immigration introduced a wide variety of European coinage to the colonies: an example was the Spanish Eight Reales which continued to circulate with official sanction until 1857. There was neither monetary policy nor control over value, counterfeits or finance; with the absence of an articulated local currency the problem of small change was acute.

see page 224

England chose to ignore the monetary plight of her colonists. The settlers eventually took action, and authority to mint coinage was granted by the General Court of Massachusetts Bay Colony. A goldsmith, John Hull, was appointed to strike an autonomous issue. He prepared planchets by melting down Spanish American coin and levied a brassage of 1/- for every forty coins he struck. The first coins produced between June and October 1652 were crude and almost blank except for the letter N E (New England) and the mark of value XII. The inadequacy of this design invited clipping and other fraudulent practices which were overcome by the introduction of the Tree coins, consisting of: the Willow Tree series (shilling, sixpence and threepence); the Oak Tree series (shilling, sixpence, threepence and twopence*); the Pine Tree series (shilling, sixpence and threepence). Hull continued to mint the coinage for thirty years with the date 1652, as in that year England was without a monarch. (Commonwealth period under Cromwell.) After the restoration of the monarchy in 1660, King Charles II lodged strong objection to the infringement of his royal prerogative, but was at a loss to prove that the coins had not been minted prior to his succession.

*The only denomination of this series not dated 1652 but 1662

1659 AD
AMERICA
Silver Sixpence
2,79 grams
21 mm diameter
Initial mark: Cross patée
Minted in London for
Cecil Calvert, the second
Lord Baltimore, for use
in his Maryland
possessions
↓

see page 225

OBVERSE: The draped bust shows Lord Baltimore in profile, left, bare-headed with long hair, encircled by the legend and a border of denticles.

CÆCILIVS : D[OMIN]V[S] :
TERRÆ-MARIÆ[QVE]* : &C.

CECIL, LORD OF EARTH AND SEA

REVERSE: The crowned shield is charged with the arms of the Baltimore family, flanked by the mark of value VI (sixpence) and encircled by the legend within a border of denticles.

CRESCITE : ET : MVLTIPLICAMINI V I

INCREASE AND MULTIPLY

In 1658 Lord Baltimore was granted an area of land in the vast unsettled North American colonies and coins bearing his effigy were sent to the Secretary of State for the Colony, Lord Baltimore's brother, Philip. This series is comprised of four denominations: shilling, sixpence, fourpence (Silver Groat) and a copper penny (Denarium).

*Spelling error on coin, should be MARISQVE

168

OBVERSE: The shield is emblazoned with the compounded arms of the Duchy of Brunswick-Wolfenbüttel formed of eleven charges, enriched with floral ornature and surmounted by five crowned and crested helmets*. The initials R(udolph) B(ornemann) and the date 1685 flank the shield at the base and the countermarked value, 3, is at eight o'clock. The coin is encircled by the legend and a floriated border.

D[EI]:G[RATIA]:RUDOLPH[US]·AUGUSTUS DUX BRUNS[VICENSIS]:ET LUN[EBURGENSIS]

BY THE GRACE OF GOD RUDOLPH AUGUST, DUKE OF BRUNSWICK AND LÜNEBURG

REVERSE: The young girl plays a lute which has ten strings, a split arrangement of lute-pins and a long fluted banner unfurling flamboyantly in a semicircular sweep over her head and draped over her right forearm. She wears an off-the-shoulder dress with three-quarter length sleeves and a knee-length skirt. Her simply styled hair flows stiffly behind and her head is inclined towards the right. Elegantly poised, she stands barefoot straddling a stream, her right foot on a shell, a symbol of resurrection and emblem of Aphrodite/Venus. In the background is the landscape of Lutenthal (Lute Valley), a mining town in the silver-rich Harz mountains. Above left is the sun with a halo and twenty-seven divergent rays; above right a semi-circular device with seventeen celestial rays bears the Hebrew inscription Jehovah, a symbol of divine presence. The coin is surrounded by a circle of denticles and the legend within a floriated border.

*See appendix on page 375

1666 – 1704 AD
GERMANY,
BRUNSWICK-WOLFENBÜTTEL
DUKE RUDOLPH AUGUST
Silver Triple Lösertaler
(Redeemable Thaler)

76,5 grams
76 mm diameter
Struck in Heinrichstadt
in 1685
Moneyer: Rudolph
Bornemann

↑

see page 226

TU TANDEM ABIECTAM REDDES DEUS ALME
SONORAM רבבז ⓘ ③ R B 16 85

YOU, LORD, WILL AT LAST TENDERLY MAKE WHAT HAS
BEEN DISCARDED TUNEFUL 1685

Redeemable multiple Thalers were first minted by Julius,
Duke of Brunswick-Lüneburg, in the late sixteenth century.
This skilled and imaginative financier was concerned about
the outflow of silver from his dominion and the European
monetary ills of the time, and he sought and devised a method
to control the supply, demand and retention of silver within his
realm. A large quantity of redeemable Thalers was minted
which his subjects were obliged to purchase and hoard in a
prescribed ratio to their wealth. Lösertalers, also known as
Juliuslöser, had to be produced on demand to the authorities
and their use was restricted to the payment of tax. Other
transactions, investments, payment of debts and exchange for
regular currency, etc., could be effected only upon application
to and with the approval of the Duke. In this way he partially
succeeded in establishing an officially controlled monetary
reserve, exchange control of cash flow to and from his realm,
and a tight rein on internal liquidity and fiscal policy. Upon
his demise the state coffers were left with net cash assets of
some 700 000 Thalers.

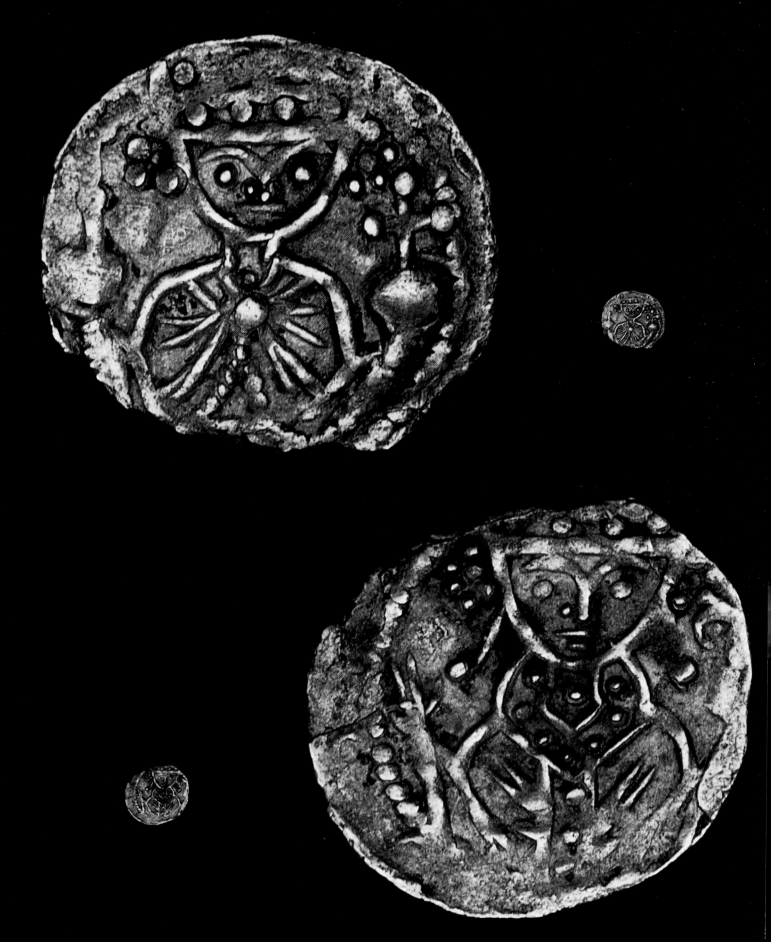

OBVERSE: The Spanish coat of arms, a cross potent forming quartered divisions, is charged with the arms of Castile and Leon, repeated diagonally. There are traces of the legend, the date and an inner border.

CAROLVS · II · D[EI] · GRATIA · HISPANIA
88°

CHARLES II BY THE GRACE OF GOD, (KING OF) SPAIN 1688

REVERSE: The vertical crowned pillars of Hercules portray the promontories which flank the Straits of Gibraltar (the narrow body of water between Spain and Africa at the entrance to the Mediterranean), once considered the western limit of the world. Their name is derived from the ancient Greek myth which tells of Hercules who, wishing to reach Gades (Cádiz), fashioned the Straits by tearing the land asunder. The pillars are traversed by two parallel lines which form nine divisions bearing the legend. The horizontal divisions in the centre proudly bear the motto "Plvs Vltra" (more beyond): testimony of Spain's pride in her conquest of the New World. The legend above, horizontally from left to right, is P (Potosí mintmark) 8 (Reales) VR (moneyer's mark), below and beneath PLVS VLTRA (moneyer's mark obliterated), the date (16) 88 and Potosí (mintmark). At the base there are three waves, traces of the legend and a patterned inner border.

1665 – 1700 AD
SPANISH AMERICA
KING CHARLES II
Silver Eight Reales –
Piece of Eight (Cob)
27,04 grams
39,8 mm diameter
Struck at the Potosí Mint
in Alto Peru (Bolivia) in
1688

POTOSI 8 VR
PLV S VL TRA
VI 1688 P[OTOS]

EL · PERV · POTOS[I] · ANO · 1688 ·

see page 227

THE PERU · POTOSÍ · IN THE YEAR 1688

Spanish conquistadores were led by Francisco Pizarro against the ill-fated Inca Empire in 1531. Subsequent occupation of the central American region brought a considerable flow of funds to Spain and her coffers were awash with gold and silver, a fact that significantly influenced world monetary history.

Mints were installed in Mexico (from 1536), Santa Fé (from 1537), Lima (from 1568), Potosí (from 1575), La Plata (in 1574 only), Cuzco (from 1698), Santiago (from 1749) and Santo Domingo (from 1530). This lucrative hive of activity brought an influx of Spanish fortune hunters to South America, pursued by a variety of eager traders of goods and services, supported by a harshly exploited native work force.

Silver bullion bars were cut into crude planchets, CABO (Cob) de BARRA – cut from a bar. The Cob was roughly remedied by being clipped, heated, then struck and its irregular size and surface produced a rude incomplete striking, characteristic of these issues. Though rough, they were widely accepted and profusely minted. This was the romantic age of buccaneers' booty and swashbuckling pirates who pillaged and plundered the European-bound galleons on the high seas, frequently relieving them of their cargo, heavily ladened with Pieces of Eight. Despite these hazards and other maritime perils, vast quantities of Cobs reached Europe. They were recoined, countermarked and reassayed into bullion bars in many countries throughout the world.

It is thought that the American dollar symbol may well have evolved from a combination of the weakly struck mark of value, 8, often appearing as an S surmounted by the two vertical lines representing the pillars of Hercules.

The Spanish Real had parity with the dollar and was widely circulated throughout America with official sanction until 1857. These Cobs were often cut into quarters by the colonists in need of small change hence the word "quarter".

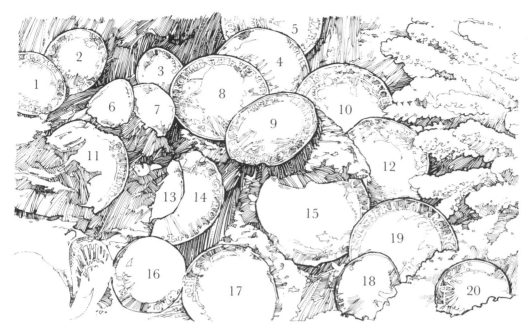

CIRCA 1702

THE WRECK OF THE
MERESTEIJN

THESE SILVER COINS FORMED PART OF THE TREASURE
RECOVERED FROM THE WRECK OF THE *MERESTEIJN*, A
DUTCH EAST INDIAMAN WHICH FOUNDERED ON THE
ROCKS IN A STORM OFF JUTTEN ISLAND, SALDANHA BAY,
CAPE OF GOOD HOPE, ON APRIL 3RD, 1702.

see pages 230, 231

The *Meresteijn* was outward bound from Amsterdam to
Batavia (Java) with a complement of troops and a consign-
ment of silver coin. Despite concerted efforts by the owners to
recover the coins, the wreck was abandoned.

In 1727 the famous English diver, John Lethbridge, was re-
tained by the Dutch East India Company to salvage ship-
wrecks at the Cape of Good Hope. His attempts to salvage
the *Meresteijn* were unsuccessful despite his proven skills
and ingenious apparatus. The treasure was destined to lie in
the custody of Davy Jones' Locker for some two and a half
centuries.

Lost for some two and a half centuries

In March 1971, Trevor Hayward, assisted by Barry Williams
of Cape Town, and inspired by local legend, located the re-

Found in 1971

mains of the wreck after a two-day search. They had great difficulty in carrying out the salvage due to wild seas and the treacherous currents in the area. Initially they found a brass signal cannon bearing the company's monogram VOC with the three Saltire crosses and A for the City of Amsterdam, and on the seabed some scattered coins of the Dutch provinces of the Spanish Netherlands in varying states of preservation. Their attention was drawn to a peculiar concretion in a rock gully and they removed a sample with the aid of a pneumatic jack hammer. They were amazed at their exciting discovery as the conglomerate was embedded with silver coin. The concretion had formed a protection around the coins and as a result many were recovered in a good state of preservation. Coins dated 1618 did not show apparent signs of wear consistent with having been in circulation, suggesting that they were used as bullion.

Exciting discovery of silver coins

As a result of the salvor's application to the Supreme Court for sole diving rights, and subsequent publicity in the newspapers, the success of the venture became common knowledge and rival treasure hunters besieged the area, preventing the systematic removal of the coins and other artifacts from the wreck. Of a representative sample of 989 coins studied by the eminent Cape Town coin expert, Dr. F. K. Mitchell, 601 were silver Ducatoons, or half Ducatoons, from the Spanish Netherlands, Antwerp, Brussels, Flanders and Liège, while 388 were silver coins of the various provinces and cities of the Dutch Netherlands.

1. Silver Arends Schelling of the Dutch city of Campen 1615
2. Silver Schelling of the Dutch province of Utrecht 1601
3. Silver Arends Schelling of the Dutch city of Zwolle 1615
4. Silver Ducatoon of Brabant – Spanish Netherlands under Philip IV – 1650
5. Silver Ducatoon of Brabant – Spanish Netherlands under Philip IV – 1650

6. Schelling?
7. Schelling?
8. Silver Ducatoon of Flanders – Spanish Netherlands under Charles II – 1694
9. Silver Ducatoon of Flanders – Spanish Netherlands under Charles II – 1673

A representative sample

10. Silver Rider of the Dutch city of Zwolle 1659
11. Silver Ducatoon of the city of Antwerp – Spanish Netherlands under Philip IV – 1639
12. Silver Rider of the Dutch province of Utrecht 1659
13. Schelling?
14. Silver Rider of the United Provinces of Holland circa 1674
15. Silver Rider, Ducatoon of the Dutch province of Zeeland 1661
16. Silver Arends Schelling of the Dutch city of Zwolle 1615
17. Silver Ducatoon of Brabant – Spanish Netherlands under Philip IV – 1634
18. Silver Arends Schelling of the Dutch city of Zwolle 1615
19. Silver Rider, Ducatoon of the Dutch province of Friesland 1660
20. Silver Arends Schelling of the Dutch city of Campen 1600

1685 – 1704 AD
GERMANY,
BRUNSWICK
WOLFENBÜTTEL
Joint rulers RUDOLPH
AUGUST and his
younger brother
ANTON ULRICH
Rudolph ruled alone
from 1666 to 1685 and
Anton ruled alone from
1704 to 1714
Silver Thaler
29,80 grams
46 mm diameter
Struck in 1692

↘

OBVERSE: The shield is emblazoned with compounded arms formed of eleven charges and surrounded by five crowned and crested armets,* flanked by the date 16 – 92. The coin is partially encircled by the legend and is surrounded by a denticular milling on the edge and on its embossed rim.

D[EI]: G[RATIA]: RUD[OLPHUS]: AUG[USTUS]: & ANTH[ONIUS]: VLR[ICH]: DD[UCES]: BR[UNSVICENSIS]: & LU[NEBURGENSIS] 16 92 **

BY THE GRACE OF GOD RUDOLPH AUGUST AND ANTON ULRICH, DUKES OF BRUNSWICK AND LÜNEBURG 1692

REVERSE: Der Wildermann (the Wildman) is portrayed as a semi-nude, full length male figure with a three-quarter facing head. His long flowing hair is garlanded with foliage; he has a long trimmed beard, drooping moustache, foliage covering his loins and appears to have breasts. He is standing on a sloped mantle of forest foliage and tears the branch of a fir tree. There is semi-circular floral orna-ture at the base and the legend is arched above finished with a denticular milling on the edge and on its embossed rim.

REMIGIO ALTISSIMI UNI

CREW OF THE HIGHEST ONE

The Wildman is probably a relic of pagan belief. This mystic savage of the forest is usually depicted as a wild, semi-nude hairy creature who sometimes holds a club and is on occasion one-eyed and grotesque. He is said to have been dumb, un-controlled when angered or lustful, and in the habit of abducting women and devouring children, especially the un-baptised. He held immense fascination and the Wildman ritual became an integral part of the Whitsuntide Festivals and frequently appeared in European medieval pagentry. He was immortalized through the rich folklore of many

*See appendix on page 375

nations, inextricably bound with sociological, physiological, metaphysical and biological connotations.

In heraldry, Wildmen were sometimes adopted as supporters and consequently appear with the coat of arms on certain coins, especially those of Germany. Sometimes, as with this specimen, the Wildman appears as the principal device and is found on the coins of Brunswick minted since 1539.

see page 228

**DD – abbreviation for the plural form Duces

OBVERSE: The facing full length figure is that of St. Peter, Patron Saint of the Bishopric. His nimbate tonsured head displays a receding hairline which is partially covered by his hair being combed forward over his forehead. He wears a long beard and a moustache, and is draped in vestments. He holds two large keys in his right hand (symbolising the keys of the Kingdom of Heaven) and a Bible in his left. There is a cartouche at his feet bearing the Arms of the Bishopric, a wheel with six spokes and a mitre. The coin is surrounded by a roped inner circle, the legend, a denticular border and a diagonally milled edge.

✠CAPITULUM CATHEDRALE OSNABRUGENSE SEDE VACANTE.

THE BISHOPRIC OF OSNABRÜCK SĒDE VACANTE*

REVERSE: Osnabrück Cathedral stands in the foreground to the right, its three spires heightened and embellished with weathercocks perched on cruciform ornaments. The spire on the left has a tulip-shaped base and there is a belfry in the tower on the right. To the left of the Cathedral are the Gertrudenberg Mountains (which appear granulated), some buildings, and a sun with sixteen rays on the horizon. Above there is an ornamental scroll which terminates in long undulating swallow tails at each end and bears the inscription.

1698 – 1715 AD
GERMANY,
OSNABRÜCK
Issued between the death of Ernest August I of Hanover (1662 – 1698) and the succession of Bishop Karl Josef of Lorraine (1698 – 1715)

*See footnote on page 194

occiduo pandunt se sidera Phœbo

THE STARS SPREAD THEMSELVES OUT IN THE WEST

Above the scroll is a constellation of twelve six-pointed stars, interspersed with thirteen smaller ones, on a reticulated background. The coin is encircled within a rope patterned inner border, the legend, a denticular border and a diagonally milled edge.

orIeiVr In tenebrIs LVX iVa et tenebra[] iVa[]erVnt sICVt MerIDIes, Isa Ia.58

THEN SHALL THY LIGHT RISE IN OBSCURITY AND THY DARKNESS BE AS THE NOON DAY – *Isaiah LXIII.10*

The Bishopric of Osnabrück was founded by Charlemagne in 804 AD and it was granted minting rights from 888. It enjoyed prosperity until the Reformation and the Thirty Years War. In 1648 it was decreed at the Peace of Westphalia that the Bishops elected should alternately be Catholic and Protestant which was the practice until 1803. The ingenious chronogram was used to record the date of this coin. It appears in Roman numerals, the sum of which amount to 1698, and are to be found interspersed in the legend of which they form an integral part.

*The See being vacant – this phrase is found on ecclesiastical coinage issued by the interim authority prior to succession of the Pope, Archbishop, Bishop, etc.

Silver Thaler
31,95 grams
41 mm diameter
Initial mark: Fleuron
Struck at Osnabrück
in 1698
↓

see page 229

OBVERSE: The snarling bear of Berne prowls on a floriated rocky crag, in profile left, within a tressure of eight scrolled arches, surrounded by the legend and a denticular milled border.

✤SENATUS·ET· SEDECIM·VIRI·REIP[UBLICAE]·BERNENSIS

THE SENATE AND COUNCIL OF SIXTEEN OF THE REPUBLIC OF BERNE

REVERSE: The arms that emerge through the clouds on either side are united by clasped hands. The left arm is vambraced and represents the Council of Sixteen that ruled Berne, and the right arm is bare with a short wide sleeve draped from its truncated shoulder, representing the Senate. Behind is a drawn sword with a long twisted handle and canine head diagonally crossed with a sceptre and garlanded above. At the apex is a stylised sun with a smiling face and twenty-one divergent rays. The coin is partly surrounded by the legend and is encircled with a denticular border.

1700 AD
SWITZERLAND,
BERNE
Silver Sechzehnerpfennig
24 grams
44 mm diameter
Initial mark: Leaf
Dies by J. L. de Beyer (B)
↓

LIBERTAS LIBERIS CURÆ 1700

LIBERTY IS THE CONCERN OF THE FREE 1700

Berne, capital of Switzerland, was founded in 1191 by Berchtold V, Duke of Zähringen as his military post and in 1218 it became a free city with an autonomous mint. For centuries the city shield has been charged with the bear, adopted as the city's mascot from which it is said the name Berne is derived. Bears have been exhibited in the city bear pits since 1513.

see page 234

1711 – 1740 AD
AUSTRIA
EMPEROR
CHARLES VI
Silver Thaler
28,82 grams
Struck in Vienna 1717
↑

see pages 232, 233

OBVERSE: The laureate bust of Charles VI, richly armoured and draped, is in profile right. The cuirass has an elaborate breast plate embossed with the elevated and displayed Austrian eagle. The pauldron(s) are truncated with floriated fringing and he has a ruffle and a gorget round his neck. The drape is edged with embroidery and is fastened with an embroidered band decorated with bows. A long luxuriant periwig covers his shoulders in a profusion of curls which lend an air of dignity to his dour corpulently jowled face. The surrounding legend appears between an inner rope pattern and concentric borders of denticles.

CAROL[VS] vi D[EI] GRATIA] RO[MANORUM]: IMP[ERATOR]: S[EMPER]: A[UGUSTUS]: HU[NGARIAE]: BO[HEMIAE] REX GER[MANIAE]: HISP[ANIAE]:

CHARLES VI, BY THE GRACE OF GOD, ROMAN EMPEROR EVER AUGUST, KING OF GERMANY, SPAIN, HUNGRY AND BOHEMIA

REVERSE: The two-headed Austrian eagle is elevated and displayed with its nimbate heads in profile, left and right, and has a crown above. It holds a drawn sword in its right talons and a sceptre in its left. It is surmounted by a cartouche bearing the crowned and quartered arms of Austria: 1 Spain, castle; 2 Hungary, patriarch's cross; 3 Bohemia, double tailed rampant lion; 4 Burgundy, bendy (or and azure); together with a crowned inescutcheon (argent) and a fess (gules). The coin is surrounded by the legend within denticular borders.

✦ARCHIDVX· AVSTRI[AE]· DVX· BVRG[VNDIAE]· COM[ES]·TYROL[IS]✦1717✦

ARCHDUKE OF AUSTRIA, DUKE OF BURGUNDY, COUNT OF THE TYROL 1717

Charles VI, the second son of Leopold I, ascended the Spanish throne during the War of Spanish Succession.

Although he was a conscientious ruler, his government became inefficient and disjointed due to his policy of provincial autonomy. His economic policy was a failure but his court was one of the most splendid in Europe. He had sumptuous palaces and Viennese culture abounded, but by contrast the provinces were extremely poor. Though he gained significant territorial acquisitions in Hungary and Serbia while at war with the Turks, these were lost at the Peace of Belgrade in 1739.

His marriage to Elizabeth Christina of Brunswick Wolfenbüttel failed to produce a son and, to ensure the succession of his daughter, Maria Theresa, he drew up his Pragmatic Sanction, a document for which he sought ratification from the European powers and which was widely confirmed. However, on his death only a few honoured their guarantees and his daughter inherited an improverished Austrian State.

OBVERSE: The laureate bust of George I in profile right has the hair coiffured with a double row of curls and luxuriant shoulder length locks which skirt the nape of the prom-ontoried truncation. The effigy is flanked by the legend within an invected border.

GEORGIUS·DEI · GRATIA · REX ·

GEORGE, BY THE GRACE OF GOD, KING

REVERSE: The Tudor rose is presented as a stylized dog rose with five outer petals edged with an ornamentally curved boss; between each of them is a sepal. The design is repeated on the inner petals and in the centre are eighteen anthers in the form of pellets. Below these crowned and united roses of York and Lancaster is a cartouche bearing a motto; above is

1723 AD
AMERICA
Struck in England for the
Plantations of the
American Colonies

201

under patent granted to
William Wood by
King George I
"Bath metal" Penny,
comprised of silver, brass
and tutenag
8,11 grams
26,5 mm diameter
Dies by Lammas, Harold
and Stanbroke
Minted at the French
Exchange, Hogg Lane,
Seven Dials, London

see page 238

the semi-circular legend; all within an invected border.

ROSA · AMERICANA · 1723   UTILE · DULCI

AMERICAN ROSE 1723   THE USEFUL WITH THE SWEET*

These plantation pieces, twopence, one penny and a half penny, were known as the Rosa Americana issue. They had a brassy gilded appearance when newly minted. A similar series was struck for use in Ireland with a different reverse. This proved most unpopular and was consequently diverted to the American Colonies. The underweight and cheap fabric of these issues proved profitable to both William Wood and the Crown; not to mention the counterfeiters, who were quick to realise the potential profits to be made and struck similar coins, known as bungtowns, which bore varied legends and therefore circumvented the counterfeit laws.

* An abbreviated form of: He hits the target who fuses the relevant/useful and the pleasurable. Horace – *Ars Poetica* 343

202

OBVERSE: The oval shield within a cartouche is embossed and emblazoned with the City Arms of Zürich and stands before a long low seat, with an ornamental diapered base, held by two confronting rampant lion supporters. The lion to the left holds a drawn sword with his extended right paw above and the lion to the right holds a palm branch. They are framed by the legend and encircled by a single inner border line, denticular border and a milled edge.

MONETA REIPUBLICÆ TIGURINÆ
COINAGE OF THE REPUBLIC OF ZÜRICH

REVERSE: This magnificent, minutely detailed city view presents a diminutive historical epitome of early eighteenth century Zürich. The river is centrally positioned on the coin with diminishing perspective and on its banks stand buildings and high steepled churches with pinnacled spires decorated with orbicular ornature, surmounted by weather vanes. A clock on the left bank edifice stands at five minutes past seven. Bridges and bastioned fortifications span the river. A ferryman rows his fare between the central tower mid-river and the right bank, while in the foreground left, a lone mariner sails towards the fortified entrance preceded by a canopied craft navigated by two bargees. An angler stands fishing from a rowing boat in the foreground right. There is a cartouche at the base of the coin bearing the date 1726 and upper left (at 10 o'clock) are the initials of the engraver HIG. The legend is arched above and there is an inner border line, a denticular border and a milled edge.

1726 AD
SWITZERLAND,
ZÜRICH
Silver Thaler
28 grams
14 mm diameter
Dies by Hans-Jakob
Gessner (HIG)
Minted at the City Mint,
Zürich

see page 235

DOMINE CONSERVA NOS IN PACE (1726)
LORD PRESERVE US IN PEACE 1726

The town of Zürich was known during Roman times and in 1238 was granted autonomous minting rights and coined regular and extensive issues. The contemporary city of Zürich remains unscathed by war due to the Swiss policy of neutrality and many of the old structures still stand.

OBVERSE: The armour clad rider, in profile left,* grasps the reins of his prancing mount with his left hand as he charges, sword at the ready. The visor of his plumed helm is raised and the ends of his sash fly behind. The hindlegs of his spirited horse are on a short corrugated groundline to the right. His steed has a luxuriant flamboyant tail and is bedecked with an ornately tooled and fringed saddle. The crowned shield below bears the arms of Westfrisia. The coin is surrounded by the legend within a denticular border.

✣ MON[ETA]: FŒD[ERATORUM]: BELG[ICORUM]: PRO[VINCIORUM]: WESTF[RISIA]: IN USUM SOCIET[ATIS]: IND[IAE]: ORIENT[ALIS]

MONEY OF THE PROVINCES OF THE NETHERLANDS, OF WESTFRIESLAND FOR THE USE OF THE EAST INDIA COMPANY

1728 AD
THE NETHERLANDS, WESTFRISIA
Struck for the Dutch East India Company, Vereenigde Oostindische Compagnie – VOC – at Hoorn under the direction of Jan Knol
Silver Ducatoon
32,97 grams
42 mm diameter
Initial mark: Turnip
↑

REVERSE: The shield bears the arms of the United Provinces. It is charged with a double-tailed rampant lion, right, who holds a bundle of arrows, one for each of the seven provinces, and brandishes a sword symbolising the motto "Unity is Strength". The shield is above an elaborate cartouche which bears the VOC monogram and is held by two magnificent lion supporters, rampant guardant, wearing coronets and poised on the upper mouldings of the cartouche. The resplendent double-arched crown, above, has a bejewelled circlet and is embellished with pearls, cruciform crest and floral ornature, and the cap has a granulated appearance. The coin is surrounded by the legend within a denticular border.

*See footnote on page 205

204

CONCORDIA RES PARVÆ CRESCUNT. 1728.

THROUGH CONCORD LITTLE THINGS GROW 1728

The Ducatoon, known as the Silver Rider, had circulated in the United Provinces since 1659. In 1728 the States General, at the request of the Dutch East India Company, agreed (subject to strict conditions) to allow various provincial mintmasters to strike Ducatoons with the company's mark for its own use in the East. These large handsome silver pieces were struck in relatively small numbers between 1728 and 1751 by the provincial mints of Holland, Zeeland, Westfrisia, Gelderland, Utrecht, Overyssel and Groningen.

see pages 236, 237

*Except for this issue of Westfrisia the rider on all Dutch Ducatoons faces right

OBVERSE: The laureate bust of George II, in profile left, has long curly locks which fall in abundant profusion. He wears a cuirass with a granulated finish over his tunic; pauldron(s) embossed with the eyes and nose of a confronting lion, edged with six granulated tabs; and a drape. The coin is flanked by the legend within a denticular border.

GEORGIVS · II DEI · GRATIA ·

GEORGE II, BY THE GRACE OF GOD

REVERSE: The four crowned shields arranged in cruciform are charged with the Arms of England and Scotland (impaled), France, Ireland and Brunswick, with the Garter Star in the centre. The legend is arranged circumferentially between the crowns and the coin is surrounded by a denticular border.

1727 – 1760 AD
GREAT BRITAIN
KING GEORGE II

205

Silver Half-Crown
14,69 grams
33 mm diameter
Struck in 1731 at the
Tower Mint
Obverse die by
John Crocker and reverse
die by John Tanner
↓

M[AGNAE]·B[RITANNIAE]·F[RANCIAE]·ET H[IBERNIAE]·
REX·F[IDEI]·D[EFENSOR]·B[RUNSVICENSIS] ET·
L[UNEBURGENSIS]·D[UX]·S[ACRI]·R[OMANI]·
I[MPERII]·A[RCHI]·T[HESAURIUS]·ET·E[LECTOR]·17 3J

KING OF GREAT BRITAIN, FRANCE, AND IRELAND,
DEFENDER OF THE FAITH, DUKE OF BRUNSWICK AND
LÜNEBURG, ARCH TREASURER AND ELECTOR OF THE
HOLY ROMAN EMPIRE 1731

see page 255

George II enjoyed wider acceptance than his father, a Hanoverian who inherited the throne of England on the death of
Queen Anne. George, unlike his father, spoke English, and
was the last British monarch to lead an army into battle. His
policies were greatly influenced by his Queen who, on occasion, led him to act against the advice of his ministers. It was
during his reign that English colonisation of Canada and
India took place and the Jacobite Rebellion was finally
quelled in 1746 by the Duke of Cumberland.

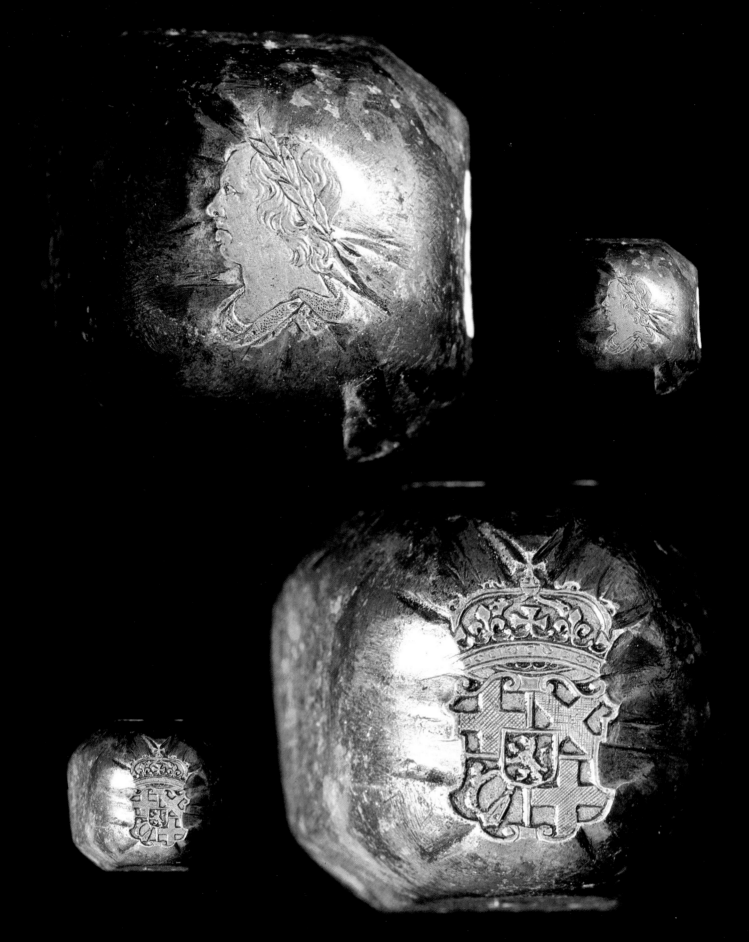

OBVERSE: The conjoined terrestrial globes are poised on the craggy promontories of the Gibraltar Straits, surmounted by the magnificent Spanish crown and flanked by the crowned pillars of Hercules which are adorned with ornate capitals and entwined with scrolls bearing the motto: PLUS ULTRA (more beyond). The coin is surrounded by the legend, punctuated with floriated stops, a denticular border and a deckled edge.

✿ VTRAQUE VNUM ✿ İM ✿ 1757 ✿ İM PLUS ULTRA

ON EITHER SIDE, ONE   IM   1757   LM   PLUS ULTRA

REVERSE: The ornate shield is emblazoned with the Spanish Arms. The first and third quarters are each charged with the triple towered castle of Castile and the second and fourth quarters with the crowned salient lion of Leon. On the middle base is the pomegranate of Granada. The inescutcheon displays the fleurs-de-lis of Bourbon and the shield is surmounted by the resplendent Spanish crown which has a bejewelled circlet with scrolled and floriated cusps and two pearled arches depressed under a cruciform crested mound. To the left in the field are the moneyer's initials JM embellished with a flower above and below; to the right the mark value 8 (Reales) is similarly embellished with flowers. The coin is surrounded by the legend, a denticular border and a deckled edge.

1746 – 1760 AD
SPANISH AMERICA
KING FERDINAND VI
Silver Eight Reales
26,89 grams
38 mm diameter
Struck at Lima,
Peru in 1757
Mintmark:
Obverse – Lima
Moneyer's initials: JM
↑

✿ FERD[I]N[AN]D[VS] · VI · D[EI] · G[RATIA] ·
HISPAN[IA] · ET IND[IAE] · REX

FERDINAND, BY THE GRACE OF GOD, KING OF SPAIN AND INDIA

see pages 256, 257

This design was introduced to restore public confidence in the Cob, which had been plagued by successive debasements and scandals in 1616 and again from 1649 to 1651. (See pages 187/188)

1760 – 1820 AD
BRITAIN
KING GEORGE III
Copper "Cartwheel" Penny
28,57 grams
35 mm diameter
3,5 mm depth
Pattern by Conrad
Heinrich Küchler
Struck at the Soho Mint,
Birmingham, under the
direction of Matthew
Boulton in 1797
↓

see pages 258, 259

OBVERSE: The bust of George III in profile right is struck in high relief. His hair is swept back from his receding forehead, displaying a widow's peak and curls on the top of his head. He is wreathed with laurel, ten leaves and five berries to view, tied with a ribbon which spirals at the nape of his neck and from which luxuriant ringlets fall, cascading over his shoulders and skirting the truncation. His ear is partially concealed by a double row of artificial-looking curls, beneath which hang long locks which grace the side of his neck. He has a prominent nose and upper lip, weak double chin with jowls, and protruberant eyes. The effigy is contained and protected by a broad embossed rim which bears an incuse semi-circular legend and has a plain edge.

GEORGIUS III · D[EI] : G[RATIA] · REX.

GEORGE III, BY THE GRACE OF GOD, KING

This specimen is one of a variety of patterns struck for the issue which were minted with diverse metals and with plain or artificially patinated finishes. This example, though not patinated, has toned with time and appears bronzed but for its beautiful bluish tinge.

REVERSE: Britannia is seated on a craggy rock in mid-ocean facing left. Her hair is elegantly contained, adorned with a diadem and a long tress flows from the nape of her neck. She wears a long dress with a high waistline, draped skirt and a crossed-over bodice, with a brooch on her sleeveless left shoulder. Curiously, her right shoulder is covered with a short sleeve. She wears open sandal(s). In her right hand Britannia holds out an olive sprig which has eleven leaves and in her left hand is a trident which rests against her forearm. There is an oval shield at the diagonal, heraldically coloured, propped against the rock. Its azure field is charged with the fimbriated saltire cross of St. Andrew (argent), surmounted by the fimbriated cross of St. George (gules). On the horizon is a triple masted man-of-war with ensign flying. The group is contained within a broad embossed rim which bears an incuse legend and has a plain edge.

BRITANNIA. 1797   (SYMBOL OF) BRITAIN 1797

George III, descendant of the Hanoverian line, was a popular monarch and enjoyed a long reign during which England underwent dramatic change. The industrial revolution and the victories of Nelson and Wellington contributed to her dominance in Europe.

Failure by the government to provide adequate copper coin, or to recognise the necessity for small change, produced an intolerable situation which was met by resourceful traders throughout England who were obliged to strike their own trade tokens. These were widely issued and usually bore an inscription and/or illustration advertising the goods and services, together with a declaration of its convertibility to coin of the realm. These tokens provide a fascinating insight into life in England during this period. Though tokens were usually issued by traders in good faith, their lack of intrinsic worth (combined with the failure of the authorities to enforce the Counterfeit Act of 1742 effectively, and public apathy in readily accepting unofficial coin), created a breeding ground for counterfeiters and profiteers. The 1770-1775 official issue virtually disappeared having been recoined into lightweight counterfeits and according to the mint report of 1787 a mere eight per cent of coin in circulation was official. The eminent industrialist, Matthew Boulton, sought to remedy the monetary plight of the nation by:
a) producing coins in abundance that were difficult and unprofitable to counterfeit;
b) producing coinage of an intrinsic value proportionate to its metallic content less a nominal brassage;

241

c) maintaining a consistent diameter through the use of a retaining collar during striking;

d) producing coins with a robust broad rim to protect their embossed type from the rigours of circulation; and

e) producing coins with an incuse inscription on the rim in order to protect them from wear and to prevent the coin from being clipped or shaved without detection.

His collaboration with the Scots engineer, James Watt, produced a steam driven minting press and his aims became a reality. After active minting of coin for the East India Company and others they were subsequently awarded a government contract to mint official copper coinage from 1797.

1760 – 1820 AD
BRITAIN
KING GEORGE III
Copper Pattern
"Cartwheel" Penny

OBVERSE: The small bust of George III in profile right is struck in relief. His hair is swept back from his receding forehead with curls on the top of his head. He is wreathed with laurel, eleven leaves and three berries to view, tied with a ribbon. Abundant ringlets fall to his shoulders and the side of his neck is graced with long locks. His ear is partially concealed by curls. He has a prominent nose and upper lip, weak double chin, jowls and protruberant eyes. The drape on the effigy is fastened by a brooch which has a jewelled roundel with eight pearls to view. Below, on the edge of the truncation, is the initial K(üchler). The bust is contained within a broad embossed rim which bears an incuse legend arched above, and at its base are two splayed olive sprigs, with sixteen leaves and five olives, tied with a ribbon which is looped above and bears the inscription M(atthew) B(oulton). It is embellished on either side with a cinquefoil. The coin has an artificial patina of a reddish hue produced from pre-patinated bronzed blanks, introduced by Matthew Boulton.

GEORGIUS III·D[EI]:G[RATIA]·REX.

GEORGE III, BY THE GRACE OF GOD, KING

REVERSE: Britannia, her head in profile left, wears a plumed Corinthian helmet and is seated on a globe which stands on an exergual ground line of rugged rocks which bears the initial K(üchler). She is invested in a chiton, draped from her right shoulder revealing her bared left breast, and has a long full skirt edged with a frilled border. The himation fastened at her right shoulder is draped across her back, over her left upper arm and her hand, which supports the oval shield propped against the globe, its azure field charged with the fimbriated saltire cross of St. Andrew (argent), surmounted by the fimbriated cross of St. George (gules). In her left hand she holds a branch, bearing sixteen olives, the stem of which is partially obscured by the shield. She grasps an upright trident with her extended right hand. On the horizon is a man-of-war with three masts and flags flying. In the exergue is the date 1797. The coin is contained within a broad embossed rim with a plain edge which bears the legend above. Below on either side are floral ornaments and at the base of the coin are two splayed olive branches, with twenty-three leaves and seven olives, tied with a ribbon looped above and bearing the name of the mint, Soho.

BRITANNIA.1797 (SYMBOL OF) BRITAIN 1797

29,25 grams
35 mm diameter
3,3 mm depth
Struck at the Soho mint, Birmingham in 1797 under the direction of Matthew Boulton from dies by Conrad Heinrich Küchler

see pages 260, 261

1762 – 1796 AD
RUSSIA
EMPRESS
CATHARINE THE
GREAT, AUTOCRAT
OF ALL THE
RUSSIANS
Copper Five Kopeks
50 grams
43 mm diameter
Struck in 1787 at
Tauritscheskaia Mint
Feodosia (Crimean
Peninsula)
Mintmark: TM

see page 262

OBVERSE: The imperial double headed eagle has its wings elevated and displayed, and between its crowned profile heads is a crown. It holds a sceptre with its right talons and an orb with its left. Its breast is surmounted by a shield charged with St. George slaying the dragon, the Arms of the Moscow government, encircled by the collar of the order of St. Andrew with badge pendant which is worn around the necks of the eagle. Its tail feathers are flanked by the mint-mark TM and at the base is a semi-circular scroll inscribed with the value. The coin has a denticular border and an obliquely milled edge.

Т М   ПЯТЬ · КОПѢЕКЪ   TM FIVE KOPEKS

REVERSE: The monogram – E(KATHERINA) I(MPERA-TRIX) II – has the imperial crown above and is flanked on either side by the date 1787, wreathed with laurel and palm, tied at the base with a looped ribbon and surrounded by a denticular border and an obliquely milled edge.

   EI II 1787

Catharine II, born Sophia of Anhalt-Zerbst, a German princess, was betrothed to Peter III of Russia. Their marriage was an unhappy one due to his mental instability. However, she followed her destiny with enthusiasm displaying Russian patriotism by joining the Orthodox Church and taking a Russian name. When her husband became Emperor she engineered his overthrow and murder and ruled Russia with ruthless efficiency and cunning. She adopted his policies of modernisation and Western methods and extended the Russian Empire. She was cultured, intelligent, of ample proportions and, it was said, enjoyed successive love affairs.

OBVERSE: The conjoined busts are of Maria and Pedro in profile right. Maria wears her hair severely combed back from her forehead revealing a widow's peak. She has tight curls and a laurel wreath tied with a ribbon at the nape of her neck. Her hair, tressed from the crown, falls softly on her shoulders and terminates in ringlets. The neckline of her dress is edged with lace, her drape is fastened with jewelled brooches and she is bedecked with pendant earrings.

The laureate bust of Pedro portrays him with his hair combed severely back and with a double chin. He wears a square-necked embellished breast plate and high collar with a ruched bib. Beneath the bust of Maria is the date 1779; the legend is arranged circumferentially above and the coin is encircled by a denticular border.

MARIA · I · ET · PETRUS · III · D[EI] · G[RATIA] · PORT[UGALIS] · ET · ALG[AVAE] · REGES. 1779

MARIA I AND PEDRO III, BY THE GRACE OF GOD MONARCHS OF PORTUGAL AND ALGAVE 1779

REVERSE: The shield is within an elaborate cartouche embellished with scroll, scallop and floral designs, and garnished with ears of corn. It is charged with the compounded arms of Portugal comprised of the heraldically coloured bordure of Castile (gules), surmounted by seven towers. This bordure commemorates the marriage of Alphonso III to the daughter of Alphonso the Wise of Castile in 1252. The escutcheon (argent) is emblazoned in cruciform with five shields (azure), each with five roundels arranged in a saltire. They represent the five wounds of Christ by whose strength Alphonso Henriques gained victory over the five Moorish princes in 1139 at the battle of Quirique. The cartouche is surmounted by the royal crown which has a jewel encrusted circlet, alternately floriated cusps, cap and a splayed double arch bedecked

1777 – 1786 AD
PORTUGAL
QUEEN MARIA I AND
HER KING CONSORT
PEDRO III
Gold Four Escudos
14,34 grams
32 mm diameter
Struck at Casa da Moeda
Mint, Lisbon 1779

see page 264

with pearls and depressed under a cruciform crested mound. The coin is encircled by a denticular border.

This regal group shows the strong family resemblance between the Queen and her uncle to whom she was married. She became insane after his death in 1786 and her son Don Juan assumed control.

1740 – 1807 AD
INDIA, MADRAS
PRESIDENCY
Gold Madras Current or
Star Pagoda
3,38 grams
10 mm diameter
Struck by the East India
Company at the Fort St.
George mint in Madras

see page 265

OBVERSE: The half-length facing deity with a convex-con-vexo head-dress has a cruciform arrangement of pellets on either side (possibly representing Vishnu and a formalisation of Brahma and Siva).
Vishnu, the beneficient preserver, is second in the Hindu Trimurti or Triad, the other two being Brahma, the power of creation, and Siva, the power of destruction.

REVERSE: The convex planchet embossed with a five-pointed star in the centre is surrounded by a granular border of pellets which form five concentric circles. The development of this design evolved from the granulated reverse of the earlier Dutch pagoda and the French adaptation which included a crescent symbol on its central boss.
Indo-European coinage goes back at least as far as the conquest of Alexander the Great. In 1498 the navigator Vasco da Gama reached India and for a time the Portuguese monopolised Indo-European trade. In the seventeenth century rival companies from the Netherlands, England, Denmark and France became active in the area. By 1640 the English East India Company had established its head-quarters at Fort St. George, Madras, on the Coromandel coast and administered Madras, Bombay and Bengal under separate presidencies. The company set up mints and like the other European traders imitated the local coinage. Probably as a means of rationalising the wide variety of Pagoda coins,

246

the East India Company changed the design in 1740/41 and the new coin became known as the Madras Current or Star Pagoda*. They were struck in great numbers and continued to be minted until 1807. These famous coins were widely copied and counterfeited in India and Europe.

This specimen is one of a number of Star Pagodas recovered in 1965 at Sea Point near Cape Town, together with other gold coins of Indian origin from the wreck of the *Fame* an English East Indiaman which ran aground on June 14th, 1822.

*The name Pagoda was borrowed from coins which bore a representation of a pagoda on the reverse

OBVERSE AND REVERSE: This piece, struck using reverse dies for both sides which appear almost identical, provides an example of a *mule*, a numismatic term applied when a pair of dies not intended for use together appear on the obverse and reverse of a coin. The VOC monogram appears as the principal device and is embellished with foliage. Beneath is the date 1756 and the coin is encircled by an outline and a dovetail patterned border.

1756 AD
THE NETHERLANDS
Copper Duit
2,81 grams
21 mm diameter
Struck in Westfrisia for the United East India Company, VOC, in 1756 under the direction of Teunis Kist
Mintmark: A cock with a rosette on either side
↑

see page 263

247

1794 AD
THE NETHERLANDS
Copper Duit
2,94 grams
22 mm diameter
Struck in Utrecht in
1794 for the United East
India Company, VOC
Mintmark: The arms of
Utrecht with a pellet on
either side
↑

see page 263

OBVERSE: The crowned Arms of Utrecht held by two rampant lion supporters are parted bendwise (argent and gules), and rest on a mound centrally positioned on a voided ground line. The exergue is embellished with scrolled ornature and the coin has a border of billets.

REVERSE: The VOC monogram appears as the principal device with the date 1794 below; above is the mintmark, the provincial Arms of Utrecht with a pellet on either side and the coin has a border of billets.

Duits were originally struck in Dordrecht in 1724 to provide adequate small change for the colonies where they were current at four to the Stuiver. However, in the Netherlands they were current at eight to the Stuiver – hence the name D'huit (one eighth, taken from the French). Though a profitable proposition to the authorities, the situation invited profiteering through private importation and exchange of Duits from the Netherlands which were used as payment for goods and services, or merely exchanged for Stuivers, in the colonies. This anomaly was circumvented by striking Duits bearing the VOC monogram for exclusive use in the colonies. These company issues were only legal tender outside the Netherlands and were struck in great quantities; from 1749 Half Duits were introduced.

OBVERSE: The splendid East Indiaman in full sail with a large flag flying at the stern, ploughs through the waves, eleven cannons to view; all within a rope circle, the legend, a denticular border and an obliquely milled edge.

INDIÆ BATAVORUM (1802)

THE INDIAS OF THE BATAVIANS 1802

REVERSE: The crowned shield of the United Netherlands is emblazoned with a crowned rampant lion facing left, holding a drawn sword and seven arrows symbolic of the united strength of the seven provinces. The shield is flanked by the mark of value I-G(uilder); all within a rope circle, the legend, a denticular border and an obliquely milled edge.

MO[NETA]: ARG[ENTA]: ORD[INUM]: FŒD[ERATORUM]: BELG[ICORUM]: HOL[LANDIÆ]: I G[ULDEN]

SILVER MONEY OF THE ORDER OF THE TREATY OF BELGIC HOLLAND

Striking of patterns in a noble metal (in this case gold instead of silver) for special occasions was an old custom in the Netherlands and was authorized by a resolution of the States General in December 1760. Similarly, Piedfort pieces (coins struck on flans of double or treble thickness) were also struck on occasions such as personal anniversaries, the introduction of a new issue, birthdays, New Year issues (Nieuwjaarspenningen), and commemorative pieces. These patterns were also presentation pieces given to mint inspectors to gain favour, but this practice was outlawed. They were struck from polished dies with great care and were not intended for general circulation.

1802 AD
THE NETHERLANDS,
THE BATAVIAN
REPUBLIC
Gold Pattern
Scheepjesgulden,
Ship Guilder
12,31 grams
32 mm diameter
Struck on behalf of the
Council of the Eastern
possessions and
settlements at Enkhuizen
under the direction of the
mintmaster
Hessel Slijper
Mintmark: Star of
Enkhuizen

↑

see page 268

1760 – 1820 AD
BRITAIN
GEORGE III

Silver Pattern Crown
25,13 grams
38 mm diameter
Dies by William Wyon
Struck at the
Royal Mint in 1817

↑

see pages 266, 267

OBVERSE: The profile head of George III, facing right, has short coiffured curls adorned with a laurel wreath, thirteen leaves and seven berries to view, tied behind with a ribbon. Below the promontoried truncation is the engraver's name W(illiam) Wyon and at the base is the date 1817. The portrait is surrounded by the legend, a recessed border of pellets, a raised rim and a plain edge.

1817 GEORGIUS III D[EI]: G[RATIA]: BRITANNIARUM REX F[IDEI]: D[EFENSOR]
1817 GEORGE III, BY THE GRACE OF GOD, KING OF THE BRITAINS, DEFENDER OF THE FAITH

This is a superb example both of William Wyon's work and of the high standard of striking achieved at the Royal Mint. The coin is struck in high relief, using various surface textures and techniques to create this spectacular effect. The face and bovine neck of this burly effigy are delicately cross-hatched in mezzotint, the hair finished with complementary granulation, and the boldly defined wreath hatched and given added dimension by the round lustrous berries, introducing yet another element of this skilful use of finishes.

REVERSE: These goddesses, the Three Graces (Charites) in classical mythology are the personification of charm, grace and beauty. They are the daughters of Zeus and Eurynome, though the identity of their mother varied in antiquity. They are Thalia (Bloom), Euphrosyne (Joy), and Aglaia (Radiance), the bestowers of beauty and charm, physically, intellectually, artistically and morally. The sisters embrace one another in a symbolic marriage of their attributes. The figure on the left stands with her back three-quarters to view in a long sleeveless chiton with a slit from the knee revealing her right leg and sandalled foot. Over her left shoulder is a himation with a border of shamrocks. Her profile head is en-

250

circled with a shamrock garland and is delicately coiffured and tied in a bun. The centre figure is draped in a long chiton with an under skirt, loose short sleeves, and a high waisted bodice with a frilled neckline. Her rose garlanded head faces left. The figure to the right is dressed in a short sleeved chiton with under skirt. Her hair is elegantly rolled around a thistle garland and held with a sphendone. They stand on an exergual ground line. To the left is the Irish harp with six strings and W. Wyon positioned diagonally. An oval shield emblazoned with the crosses of St. George and St. Andrew rests on the ground line between the left and central figures, half to view. In the field to the right is the thistle of Scotland. In the exergue is a palm branch crossed with a rudder. The coin is surrounded by the legend, a recessed border of pellets, a raised rim and a plain edge. This exquisite reverse was perhaps inspired by an ancient coin of Germa on which the Three Graces appear.

FOEDUS INVIOLABILE   **INVIOLABLE PACT**

1820 – 1830 AD
BRITAIN
KING GEORGE IV
Proof Silver Crown
28,10 grams
37 mm diameter
Struck at the Royal Mint,
Tower Hill from dies by
Benedetto Pistrucci
in 1822

see page 269

OBVERSE: The head of King George IV faces left. He has curly hair and wears a laurel wreath with thirteen leaves to view tied with a long ribbon behind. He has a burly face, prominent jowls, a double chin and a bovine neck. Below the truncation of the neck are the engraver's initials BP. The coin is surrounded by the legend, a denticular border, raised rim and an inscription embossed on its edge.

GEORGIUS IIII D[EI]: G[RATIA]: BRITANNIAR[UM]: REX F[IDEI]: D[EFENSOR]

GEORGE IV, BY THE GRACE OF GOD, KING OF THE BRITAINS, DEFENDER OF THE FAITH

REVERSE: St. George, sword at the ready, triumphs over the terrible winged dragon as it cowers beneath the hooves of his prancing mount. The Patron Saint of England, portrayed in the neo-classical style, is semi-nude and his physique is muscular and virile. He wears a helmet, greaves, a scabbard (its strap to view) and a cloak flowing flamboyantly behind. The group is positioned on a broad slab and there is a broken lance across the left corner which appears to overhang its rugged hatched edge. In the exergue is the date 1822 and to the right are the initials BP. The coin is surrounded by a denticular milling, a raised rim and an edge with an embossed inscription. This superbly engraved masterpiece is toned with sunset hues of azure, red and yellow. 1822

The legendary St. George is said to have been a Roman officer, martyred in about 300 AD near Lydda during the Diocletian persecution, who came to the aid of the early Crusaders at Antioch in 1098, presumably in some form of re-incarnation. He was adopted as the Patron Saint of England during the reign of Edward III (1327 – 1377) as he represented Christian triumph over evil.

OBVERSE: The head of King George IV facing left has luxuriant curly hair. Below is the date 1826 flanked by ornamental stops. The coin is surrounded by the legend, a denticular border, a raised rim and a milled edge. It is toned with turquoise, purple, blue and rust, tinged with gold.

GEORGIUS IV DEI GRATIA · 1826 ·

GEORGE IV, BY THE GRACE OF GOD 1826

REVERSE: The magnificent shield is emblazoned per cross with: 1 & 4 Three lions passant guardant, in pale (England); 2 A lion rampant within a double tressure flori, counter-flori (Scotland); 3 A ten-stringed harp which has a remarkable frame comprised of a nude female in semi-profile with wing(s) elevated and displayed and her hair in a bun. She is joined to the resonator at the base by scrolled ornature.

The shield is surmounted by an escutcheon of Hanover, inverted per pall, and is charged with: 1 Two lions passant guardant, in pale (Brunswick); 2 A semé of hearts and a lion rampant (Lüneburg); 3 A horse courant (Westphalia).

An inescutcheon is charged with the golden crown of Charlemagne (badge of the Arch Treasurer of the Holy Roman Empire). The escutcheon is ensigned with a crown displaying four domed arches with ornamented cusps and a jewelled circlet. The principal shield is surmounted by an ornately fashioned armet with a barred helm and an elaborate foliate lambrequin. It is ensigned with the royal crown which has a jewelled circlet heightened by alternate crosses patée and fleurs-de-lis on its cusps and two jewel encrusted arches depressed under the mound studded with pearls and roundels. Below is a granulated scroll with a plain edge bearing the motto and terminating in divided foliate embellishments. The coin is surrounded by the legend, a denticular border and a raised rim.

1820 – 1830 AD
BRITAIN
KING GEORGE IV
Silver Half-Crown
14,11 grams
32 mm diameter
Struck in 1826 at the
Royal Mint
Obverse die engraved
by William Wyon
after the bust by Sir
Francis Legatt Chantrey
Reverse die engraved by
Jean Baptiste Merlen

see pages 270, 271

The reverse of this specimen is remarkably toned; the resplendent golden hues of the shield are offset by the subdued shades of gilt and silver against a field of azure, pink, orange and magenta.

In 1824 the King appointed William Wyon to engrave new dies for a new issue based on the flattering bust by Sir Francis Chantrey because he was dissatisfied with the unflattering effigies produced by Pistrucci who refused to copy Chantrey's work.

George IV was notorious for his love affairs and extravagances. He married Queen Caroline of Brunswick whom he deserted. He acquired a vast collection of paintings and was responsible for the building of Regent Street, the Brighton Pavilion and the extensions to Windsor Castle.

BRITANNIARUM REX FID[EI]: DEF[ENSOR]
KING OF THE BRITAINS, DEFENDER OF THE FAITH
DIEU ET MON DROIT
GOD AND MY RIGHT

OBVERSE: The oval coin has a thin flat flan and is stamped at each end with the official seal, the Hanaoshi, a Kiri (*Paulownia*) flower with anthers and an intricate labyrinth of delicate tracery. It is centred within an embossed fan-shaped framework with an arched base and below the arch, bearing the calligraphic mark of value (one Ryo), is a billet-shaped stamp with an embossed border. Beneath is a similar billet-shaped stamp which bears the signature of the Mitsutsugu (Goto) family who controlled the gold mint at Yedo. There is a fimbriated pattern of horizontal cut marks on either side of the coin which terminate towards the outer ends of the billet-shaped stamps. The circular concave indents on the obverse were impressed during the stamping of the reverse.

254

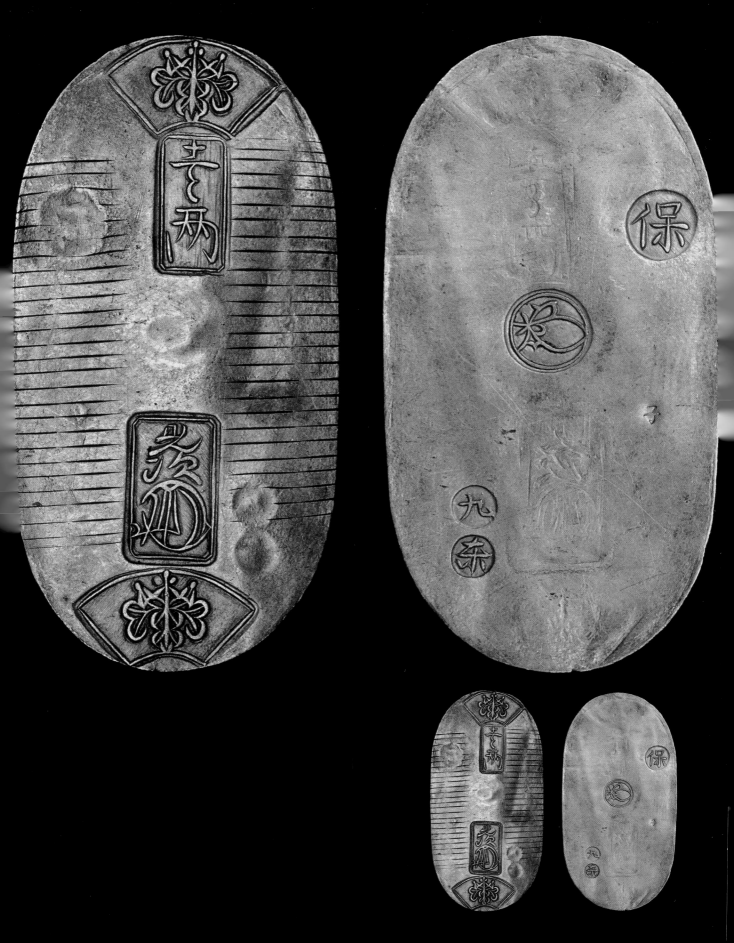

DIRIGE DEUS GRESSUS MEOS.

MDCCCXXXIX.

W. WYON R.A.

ANNO REGNI

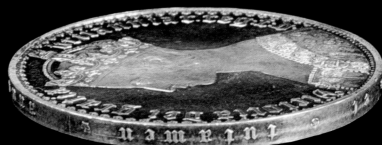

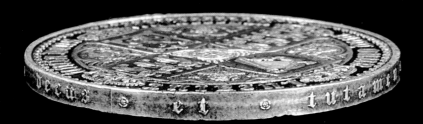

REVERSE: In the centre is the circular seal of the gold mint with an embossed surround. The stamp above to the right denotes the era and below are two vertically positioned control stamps of the mint. The specimen has a chop mark below the centre to the right. The name is derived from the Hindu *chhap*, an official assize or customs house stamp. It was an Eastern custom until recent times to stamp coinage with a personal chop mark as a guarantee of its correctness by private individuals or merchants to obviate their careful scrutiny if the coins were returned to them – reminiscent of the ancient Lydian custom.

In about 1400 AD rich gold and silver deposits were discovered on the island of Sado off the coast of north west Japan and were traded in the form of small roughly cast ingots and gold dust. The first Japanese gold coins were introduced during the Tensho era between 1573 and 1592. In about 1585 AD Toyotomi Hideyoshi, the military dictator, realised the need for an articulated currency in order to trade with the European merchants and to finance his territorial ambitions. He minted large quantities of gold coin known as Oban (large mould). These large gold coins were thin oval castings, and being of relatively high value they were not practical coins for daily use but were used as a store of value for large payments, presentation pieces and European trading. Small fractional currency followed, more suited to everyday use which included the Goryoban (five Ryo) and the Koban (one Ryo).

1830 – 1853 AD
JAPAN
TOKUGAWA
SHOGUNATE
Gold Koban, one Ryo
11,25 grams
30 x 60 mm
Minted in Yedo (Tokyo)
1837 – 1843 during the
Tempo Era

see page 272

1829 – 1837 AD
UNITED STATES OF
AMERICA
PRESIDENT ANDREW
JACKSON
Silver Quarter Dollar
6,74 grams
23 mm diameter
Engraved by William
Kneass
Issued 1831 – 1838
↓

OBVERSE: The bust of Liberty personified faces left. She has prominent features and luxuriant tressed curls which grace her neck and cascade behind, skirting the rear tip of her truncated effigy. The drape of the promontoried bust is gathered at the shoulder and fastened with a roundel. She wears a Phrygian slave cap which has a broad band bearing the Liberty inscription. In this design the apex of the conical peaked cap is folded forward and, therefore, the coin is referred to as the turban variety.

The Phrygians of the ancient Greek world, once conquered by the Lydians, did not manage to regain their independence and the name Phrygia became synonomous with slavery. However, in Roman times Phrygian caps were worn by freed slaves to signify their emancipation and came to represent Liberty.

There are seven six-pointed stars arranged radially to the left and six to the right. These stars represent the original thirteen states and were added to as each state joined the Union. Below the bust is the date 1834. The coin is surrounded by an indented raised rim and a milled edge. This specimen is toned with hues of green, azure, pink and red.

LIBERTY 1834   LIBERTY 1834

see page 273

REVERSE: The American Eagle has its wings elevated and displayed. The escutcheon on its breast is charged with the heraldically coloured Union Shield. It has thirteen vertical stripes (palewise) alternately white and red (argent and gules) representing the thirteen original colonies, and the uppermost area of the escutcheon (chief) is in azure representing Congress. The eagle grasps three arrows in its left talons and in its right talons an olive branch which signifies the nation's desire for peace while remaining ever resolute in its defence. The legend is arched above and below in the exergue is the mark of value, 25 c(ents). The coin is surrounded by an indented raised rim and a milled edge.

UNITED STATES OF AMERICA 25C

UNITED STATES OF AMERICA 25C

OBVERSE: The head of the young Queen faces left. She has wavy locks tressed from her forehead along the side of her head. Her hair is brushed back to the crown and up from the nape of her neck, elegantly braided and dressed in ringlets. Her coiffure is bound by edged fillets, one with a tracery of nine ornamental scrolls (plus half a scroll at each end partially visible) and the other is foliated and has eleven leaves (plus two partially) to view. The regal effigy is surrounded by an egg and tongue border, protected by a raised rim, and an edge with embossed letters, similarly protected.

VICTORIA D[EI]: G[RATIA]: BRITANNIARUM REGINA F[IDEI]: D[EFENSOR]:*

VICTORIA, BY THE GRACE OF GOD, QUEEN OF THE BRITAINS, DEFENDER OF THE FAITH

1837 – 1901 AD
BRITAIN
QUEEN VICTORIA
Gold Pattern Five Pounds
– Una and the Lion
29,26 grams
38 mm diameter
2,3 mm depth
Struck at the Royal Mint
from dies by William
Wyon in 1839

↑

REVERSE: This symbolic portrayal is that of the young Queen in the guise of Una guiding the magnificent British lion left. The Queen is elegantly attired in a long sleeved dress with a full trailing skirt and a high neck-line with horizontal trim and invested with the mantle of the Garter. Her coiffure is dressed from her forehead over her temples, looped round her ears and terminates in plaits, held at the back by the fillet which also binds the locks swept up from the nape of her neck. She wears a small coronet with a chased circlet which has crosses patée and fleurs-de-lis. In her right hand Una holds a sceptre which has an eagle crest, in front and to the right of the lion's head. She has a shawl draped over her arm and holds an orb in her left hand. The group is positioned on a slab and below in the

see pages 274, 275

* or D(efenstrix)

exergue is the date MDCCCXXXIX (1839) and the name of the engraver W. Wyon RA beneath. The motto is positioned radially above and the coin is surrounded by an egg and tongue border, protected by a raised rim, and an edge with embossed letters, similarly protected.

DIRIGE DEUS GRESSUS MEOS. MDCCCXXXIX.
MAY THE LORD DIRECT MY STEPS   1839

DECUS ET TUTAMEN ANNO REGNI TERTIO
AN ORNAMENT AND A SAFEGUARD IN THIRD YEAR OF THE REIGN

Una, the heroine of Edmund Spenser's *The Faerie Queen* (1590), embarks upon a series of symbolic adventures with St. George during which she is attended by a lion. This issue was not put into circulation except for the patterns, proofs and sets of 1839, possibly because of its high relief and consequent susceptibility to wear. However, the Victorians may well have considered the theme inappropriate for their young Queen.

OBVERSE: The bust of the young Queen faces left. Her hair is plaited from her temples, looped round her ears and fastened beneath her crown. The circlet of her crown is chased and bejewelled with geometrically patterned ornature, its cusps are enriched alternately with fleurs-de-lis and crosses patée and its pearl encrusted arches are heightened by a mound. Her ornate Gothic style dress of diapered brocade is embroidered with Roses of England, Shamrocks of Ireland and Thistles of Scotland. It has a square neckline fimbriated with pearls and large lace medallions ornately crocheted with quatrefoils, geometric cruciform patterns, floriate spandrels and embroidered roundels. The bodice has a softly gathered centre panel bedecked on either side with an embossed quatrefoil brooch, embellished with a square of pearls. The legend is positioned radially on either side of the bust, surrounded by a tressure of diminutive arches decorated with fleurs-de-lis, and protected by a rim and an edge with an embossed inscription.

VICTORIA, BY THE GRACE OF GOD, QUEEN OF THE BRITAINS, DEFENDER OF THE FAITH

REVERSE: The four shields are arranged in cruciform and their bases form a quatrefoil in the centre of which is the Garter Star. The shields are: 1 & 3 The three lions passant guardant in pale (England); 2 The lion rampant with a double tressure flori, counter-flori (Scotland); 4 The nine-stringed Irish harp which has a magnificent nude female figure in semi-profile with her hair in a bun and with the lower part of her figure joined to the wedge-shaped resonator by a foliated scroll, as are her wings which are elevated and displayed. Each shield is surmounted by the Royal crown with a jewelled circlet embellished with crosses patée and fleurs-de-lis alternately on each cusp, and

1837 – 1901 AD
BRITAIN
QUEEN VICTORIA
Silver Gothic Crown
28,29 grams
38 mm diameter
Struck at the Royal Mint
in 1847
Obverse die by
William Wyon
Reverse die by
William Dyce
↓

see pages 276, 277

heightened by two pearl encrusted arches elevated under the mound.

tueatur unita deus anno dom[ini] mdcccxlvii

MAY GOD GUARD THESE UNITED, IN THE YEAR OF OUR LORD 1847

William Wyon's splendid and much celebrated crown was inspired by a romantic revival of Gothic art. It is said to have been engraved at the suggestion of the Queen. Although there are many varieties of this type extant, the coin was not issued for general circulation.

Victoria, niece of William IV, ascended the throne at the tender age of eighteen. She married Prince Albert of Saxe Coburg and Gotha, and made him her Consort. They had nine children and their marriage was a blissfully happy one. She adored Albert and was much influenced by him. By her example of devotion, duty, dignity and decorum she enhanced the prestige of the monarchy.

Devastated by Albert's untimely death from typhoid in 1861 Victoria withdrew into seclusion. Ultimately she was coaxed from her seclusion by Disraeli who bolstered her morale and obtained the title of Empress of India for her in 1897. She was bold and efficient in affairs of state, and encouraged and supported a variety of endeavours. Through the marriages of her children she was related to most of the Royal Houses of Europe. Despite her unpopular period of withdrawal from public life, she was revered by a nation which overwhelmingly demonstrated its affection and loyalty for her during her Jubilees of 1887 and 1897, the latter being the occasion of her Diamond Jubilee. During Victoria's long reign, Britain prospered and became the world's most powerful empire.

decus et tutamen anno regni MDCCCXLVII

AN ORNAMENT AND A SAFEGUARD IN THE YEAR OF THE REIGN 1847

OBVERSE: Liberty, in a long sleeveless dress, is seated right with her head turned to the left, her hair in tresses falling loosely behind. In her left hand she holds a staff, on top of which rests a Phrygian slave cap. With her right hand she supports the Union Shield draped diagonally with a scroll bearing the Liberty inscription. Below in the exergue is the inscription C. Gobrecht F(ecit) – made it (from the Latin *facere* – to make) and the date 1836. The coin is surrounded by a denticular border, a raised rim and a plain edge. The obverse is not illustrated photographically.

REVERSE: The American Eagle volant, left, is surrounded by a constellation of twenty-six, six-pointed stars, respresenting the United States. The thirteen large stars represent the original colonies. The coin is encircled by the legend within a denticular border, raised rim and a milled edge.

◎ UNITED STATES OF AMERICA ◎ ONE DOLLAR

The splendent eagle, on the reverse, which has toned with a blaze of sunset hues, was inspired by the design of Titian Peale while the obverse design is after a painting by Thomas Sully.

1837 – 1841 AD
UNITED STATES OF
AMERICA
PRESIDENT ANDREW
JACKSON
Silver Pattern Dollar
26,99 grams
35 mm diameter
Struck in 1836 at the
Philadelphia Mint from
dies by Christian
Gobrecht
↓

see page 278

1842 AD
SWITZERLAND
CANTON
GRAUBÜNDEN,
CHUR

Silver Schulzentaler,
Shooting Thaler,
Four Swiss Francs
28,3 grams
39 mm diameter
Struck in Munich from
dies by the Swiss die
engraver Nett for the
Confederate Rifle
Competition of 1842
in Chur
↓

see page 279

OBVERSE: The three oval cartouches are entwined by a ribbon which is held by three hands clasped together surrounded by celestial rays with forearms emerging through the clouds above. These are symbolic of the divine presence of the Trinity which unites the Republic of the three leagues. The fimbriated heraldically coloured shield on the left is that of Ober Bund*, the highlands in the Vorder Rhine Valley, charged palewise argent and sable, crested with a demi, armour clad knight facing who holds a spear at the diagonal offset against an azure field. The central cartouche bears the charge of the Gotteshausbund (God's house league) which was formed by The City and Chapter of Chur and the subjects of its powerful bishopric – a sable steinbock (the alpine ibex) salient on an argent field. To the right is the cartouche of Zehngerichtenbund (the league of the Ten Jurisdictions). The shield is divided quarterly one and four azure, and two and three or, surmounted by a counter coloured cross bound saltirewise at the centre. It has a confronting half-length bearded male crest holding the Zehngerichtenbund banner and the tree of life (fir of Woden), and is offset against an azure field. There are crossed oak branches below and the coin is encircled by a border line, the legend protected by a denticular border, a raised rim and an inscribed edge: Eintracht Macht Stark – Unity is strength.

❈ CANTON GRAUBUNDEN ❈ 4 SCHWEIZER FRANKEN   4 SWISS FRANCS

REVERSE: The shield bearing the Swiss emblem is heraldically coloured, its field gules, and is charged with a Greek cross argent. The shield is surmounted by a triple-plumed hat, and a powder horn is suspended from the two tasselled ties at the base of the shield. There are four flag poles crossed diagonally behind the shield, their flags partially visible. To the left and right respectively are branches of oak and laurel.

*Often referred to as the "Grey League"

294

The coin is encompassed by an inner border line, the legend, a denticular border, raised rim and an inscribed edge.

EIDGENÖSSISCHES FREISCHIESSEN IN CHUR 1842

CONFEDERATE RIFLE COMPETITION IN CHUR 1842

This Shooting Thaler is typical of those issued in Switzerland at shooting festivals. The coin is superbly engraved and struck. The hatching and cross-hatching is skilfully incorporated in the design to signify the heraldic colouring.

In 1799 the three leagues were incorporated into the Helvetic Republic and in 1803, under the name of Canton of the Grisons or Graubünden, became a full member of the reconstituted Swiss Confederation.

OBVERSE: The effigy of President Burgers faces to the left. His hair is brushed back and he has a moustache and a long beard which falls below his draped and truncated neck. At the base is the date 1874. The legend is arched radially above and the coin is surrounded by denticles, an embossed rim and a milled edge.

1872 – 1877 AD
SOUTH AFRICAN
REPUBLIC,
TRANSVAAL
PRESIDENT THOMAS
FRANÇOIS BURGERS
Gold Staatspond,
one Sovereign
7,98 grams
22 mm diameter
↓

THOMAS FRANÇOIS BURGERS 1874

REVERSE: The cartouche embellished with scrolls, bears an oval shield charged with the Arms of the South African Republic. In the three divisions are: 1 A lion couchant argent on a field, gules, facing to the right; 2 A full length bearded Boer argent facing, against an azure field, wearing long trousers, a short sleeved shirt and a hat, holding a crooked stick in his left hand; 3 An outspanned covered ox wagon

Dies by L.C. Wyon, engraver at the Royal Mint Struck by Ralph Heaton & Sons, Birmingham, England, from alluvial gold acquired from the newly discovered gold fields (1873) at Pilgrims Rest in the Lydenburg District of the Transvaal

see page 280

argent with a single shaft facing left on a rugged ground against a field, vert.

There is an angular inescutcheon argent with a convergent base charged with an anchor. An eagle with its wings elevated and displayed is perched on the cartouche above. There are six unfurled fimbriated flags flanking the shield, their poles capped with ferrules crossed diagonally behind. They represent the flag of the South African Republic, known as the *Vierkleur* (four colours: red, blue, green and white).

There is an indented scroll below bearing the legend and beneath is a single pellet. The legend is arched above and the coin is surrounded by a denticular border, an embossed rim and a milled edge.

ZUID AFRIKAANSCHE REPUBLIEK
SOUTH AFRICAN REPUBLIC
EENDRAGT MAAKT MAGT   UNITY IS STRENGTH

A petition to the Volksraad (Parliament) in 1853 called for the minting of the first indigenous coinage, but it was not until 1874 that action was taken. Finally, President Burgers proudly presented fifty Staatsponden for formal approval and acceptance as legal tender. The astonished and evidently unpopular head of state excited furore in the Volksraad, many of whose members criticized and chided him for his efforts. They considered the obverse design egotistic and it was officially accepted only after protracted and acrimonious debate. A mere 837 coins were struck of which 142 are of the coarse beard variety.

The South African Republic (Transvaal) was annexed by Britain in 1877.

296

OBVERSE: The bust of Queen Victoria faces to the left, her head is partly covered by a long veil, edged with lace secured by a double layered ruffled head band with a peak. She wears a small crown perched on her head. It has an ermine lined circlet chased with a plain band and cusps ornamented with crosses patée and fleurs-de-lis. There are two pearl encrusted arches with seventeen pearls to view heightened by a mound. The bodice of her dress is edged with a broad lace lined collar. The Queen is adorned with a pearl pendant and earring(s), the Garter Star and the Badge of the Imperial Order of the Crown of India. On the truncation are the initials J(oseph) E(dgar) B(oehm). The bust is flanked by the legend positioned radially on either side and is surrounded by a denticular border, an embossed rim and a milled edge.

This dignified, lifelike portrayal is toned with hues of turquoise, pink and gold. However, the diminutive crown perched on the head of the Queen has attracted much adverse criticism.

VICTORIA D[EI]: G[RATIA]:
BRITT[ANNIARUM]: REG[INA]:
F[IDEI]: D[EFENSOR]:

VICTORIA, BY THE GRACE OF GOD, QUEEN OF THE BRITAINS, DEFENDER OF THE FAITH

REVERSE: St. George, sword at the ready, triumphs over the terrible winged dragon as it cowers beneath the hooves of his prancing mount. The Patron Saint of England, portrayed in the neo-classical style, is semi-nude and his physique is muscular and virile. He wears a helmet, greaves, a scabbard (its strap to view) and a cloak flowing flamboyantly behind. The group is positioned on a broad slab and there is a broken lance across the left corner which appears to overhang its rugged hatched edge. In the exergue is the date 1887 and to

1837 – 1901 AD
BRITAIN
QUEEN VICTORIA
Silver Crown
28,36 grams
38 mm diameter
Struck at the Royal Mint
in 1887 on the occasion
of Queen Victoria's
Golden Jubilee
The obverse die was
adapted from a Jubilee
Commemorative medal,
modelled from life, by
Sir Joseph Edgar Boehm
The reverse die is by
Benedetto Pistrucci
originally designed
in 1816
↓
see page 281

the right are the initials BP. The coin is surrounded by denticular milling, a raised rim and an embossed edge.

1857 – 1860 AD
UNITED STATES OF
AMERICA
PRESIDENT JAMES
BUCHANAN
Gold Ten Dollars
16,70 grams
26 mm diameter
Struck from dies by
Christian Gobrecht
↓

see page 284

OBVERSE: The bust of Liberty personified faces to the left. Her hair is coiffured with Attic elegance and it is arranged in a tri-formed bun adorned with pearls. She wears an arched coronet with a broad concave circlet and embossed edge. It is heightened at the front and displays the Liberty motto. Below the coronet is a band of curls and her neck is graced with two ringlets, one falls from behind her ear and the other on the nape. Beneath the arched truncation is the date 1859. The effigy is surmounted by thirteen six-pointed stars (representing the thirteen original colonies), and is protected by a denticular border, embossed rim and a milled edge.

REVERSE: The displayed American Bald Eagle has the Union Shield on its breast. It is heraldically coloured, the charge is comprised of thirteen vertical stripes (palewise) alternately white and red (argent and gules) and a blue (azure) chief.
The magnificent bird displays a formidable hooked beak and a beady eye. In its right talons it holds a long-stemmed olive branch with six leaves and three berries to view, and in its left talons three arrows with short shafts, large barbs, and long feathered flights.
The eagle is encircled by the legend and protected by a denticular border, embossed rim and a milled edge.

◦ UNITED STATES OF AMERICA ◦
TEN D[OLLARS]

298

OBVERSE: The head of Liberty personified faces right. She wears a Phrygian slave cap, the apex of which is folded forward, and a laurel wreath, seventeen leaves and three berries to view, with ties which terminate in swallow tails flamboyantly arranged at the nape of her neck. On the hair above her forehead is a band bearing the liberty inscription. The initial B(arber) appears on the left of the truncation and beneath is the date 1910. The effigy is flanked by thirteen six-pointed stars positioned radially, six to the left and seven to the right, representing the thirteen original colonies, and above is the motto. The coin is protected by a denticular border, embossed rim and a milled edge, and is toned with golden hues.

IN GOD WE TRUST 1910

REVERSE: The American Bald Eagle, the national bird of the United States, is displayed and has the Union Shield emblazoned on its breast, heraldically coloured with thirteen vertical stripes (palewise) alternately white and red (argent and gules) and a blue (azure) chief. In its beak is a flowing scroll bearing the motto.

E·PLURIBUS UNUM   **ONE FROM MANY**

The eagle holds an olive branch with thirteen leaves in its right talons and in its left a bundle of thirteen arrows symbolising strength in unity; above is a constellation of thirteen five-pointed stars representing the thirteen original colonies. The coin is surrounded by the legend and protected by a denticular border, embossed rim and a milled edge.

UNITED STATES OF AMERICA HALF DOLLAR

The reverse die is engraved after the style of the Great Seal. The eagle which appears on coins after 1855 is referred to

1909–1913 AD
UNITED STATES OF AMERICA
PRESIDENT
WILLIAM HOWARD TAFT
Silver Half Dollar
12,49 grams
30 mm diameter
Struck in 1910 from dies by Charles E. Barber

see pages 282, 283

officially as Peter the Mint Bird. This legendary mascot and mint engraver's model, it appears, chose to roost on the Philadelphia mint in the late 1840s where he was cared for and given free access. His sudden demise was a result of his preoccupied curiosity with a coin press; however he continues to reside and model there, stuffed and mounted in a glass case.

The eagle device is required by law to appear on all United States coinage of a denomination higher than a Dime.

Photography is the process by which an image is recorded, through the formation of a latent image produced by the action of light on photo-sensitized material, which is then developed and fixed chemically. The following section deals with its origins and principles as applied to coin photography.

The Evolution of the Photographic Process

Camera obscura

The principle of the camera obscura was known to Arab scholars as early as the eleventh century and later scientifically described by Leonardo da Vinci in 1500. This principle involved the use of a dark enclosure with a single small aperture at one end through which light passed, projecting an inverted image of the view outside on its inside wall.

Light sensitive chemicals

In 1727, T. H. Schulze recorded experiments with silver chloride, a compound darkened by exposure to light.

Recording of photographic image

Around 1800, Thomas Wedgwood (1771 – 1805), the youngest son of the famous potter, succeeded in recording a photographic image by coating paper or leather with silver nitrate or silver chloride. He then placed certain objects, such as leaves, lace and paper patterns, in contact with the coating, and exposed them to sunlight. He was unable, however, to fix the image which after a short while lost its permanence.

Images recorded in a camera

Joseph Nicéphore Niepce (1765 – 1833) introduced the use of light sensitive bitumen on metal or glass. He then applied this principle to the camera and succeeded in recording images. This process was of little practical value, however, being cumbersome and indistinct and requiring hours of exposure. The work of Monsieur Niepce came to the attention of a fellow countryman, Louis Jacques Mande Daguerre (1787 – 1851), with whom he co-operated until his death in 1833.

Development of latent image

By 1839, Daguerre had invented a practical photographic process, Daguerrotype, details of which were announced in August of that year. His process consisted of a copper sheet, silver plated and polished, which was made light sensitive by fuming it with iodine. The vapour from the iodine reacted with the silver to produce silver iodide.When exposed in the camera a latent image was formed by the blackening of the light sensitive silver iodide coating. This latent image was developed by fuming the sensitized sheet with mercury. The last stage was to fix it by dissolving the unblackened areas in sodium thiosulphate (hypo). Daguerrotypes were widely praised for their ability to record fine detail and for their tonal range. However, there were certain drawbacks to this process as each plate was unique with no known way of producing copies. Some found the glare from the highly polished surface hard on the eye, and the image had a tendency to appear as a negative if viewed from certain positions. Daguerrotypes continued to be used for approximately a decade.

Around the time of the Daguerrotype, John Frederick William Herschel (1792 – 1871) suggested to his friend and fellow scientist, William Henry Fox Talbot, the use of sodium thiosulphate as a means of removing the unexposed light sensitive chemicals; thus fixing the photographic image. Herschel was the first to introduce the word photography and the terms negative and positive in a photographic context. *Fixing of permanent image*

Fox Talbot succeeded in producing a permanent negative through a camera, known as a Talbotype, and later introduced a negative/positive process, Calotype, employing silver iodide (or silver chloride) and paper, and using liquid chemicals to develop the latent image. After several reductions in exposure time were achieved, practical portraiture became feasible. The paper negatives of the Calotype had their shortcomings, however, because the light transmitted through them was partially obscured by the fibre of the paper, producing a poorly defined image. To minimise this problem the translucency was increased by applying a wax coating. The Daguerrotype, however, remained superior in image quality. *Negative/positive process*

In 1840 a special photographic lens, designed to function with a large aperture, was made by Joseph Max Petzval (1807 – 1891). This, too, helped to shorten exposure times dramatically, making portrait photography popular. *Photographic lens*

The Calotype was superseded in 1852 when Frederick Scott Archer (1813 – 1857) developed the wet collodion plate; the first practical process for making glass negatives. He combined the application of the glass plate base (introduced by a cousin of Niepce) with the discovery of collodion by Louis *Glass negatives*

303

Menard and the idea of its role in photography by Robert Bingham. Scott Archer's process consisted of an iodised collodion-coated glass plate which had been sensitized in a solution of silver nitrate, exposed immediately when wet and then developed. Though very inconvenient, it produced superior results and shorter exposure times.

Gelatin based film

Richard Leach Maddox (1816 – 1902) described the making of a film emulsion utilizing a gelatin solution prepared from cattle bones into which silver bromide was precipitated. This emulsion was coated and dried prior to its use and could be stored for months whilst retaining its sensitivity. It then became normal practice for photographers to buy photographic plates, instead of making their own. This great advance was the forerunner of modern film.

Colour process described

In May 1861 James Clerk Maxwell demonstrated a colour process. It was of poor quality, and although it was later extended by du Hauron and Cros, was not commercially viable.

Increased spectral sensitivity

Photographic materials responded to ultra-violet and blue light. In 1873, Hermann Wilhelm Vogel (1834 – 1898) extended the colour sensitivity of photographic film by adding small quantities of dies to the emulsion, thereby increasing the sensitivity of the film to most of the visual colour spectrum: orthochromatic. He later increased it to cover virtually the whole of the visual colour spectrum: panchromatic.

Roll film service introduced

An enterprising American, George Eastman, produced an inexpensive and less cumbersome method by introducing a camera in 1888, which he supplied loaded with sufficient film to produce 100 pictures. After taking the photographs, the camera (together with the enclosed film) was sent back to Eastman's company for developing and printing. The camera was then reloaded and returned to its owner. This service captured the imagination of the general public and enabled everyone to try his hand at photography. Kodak's popular slogan ''you press the button and we do the rest'' was to become legend.

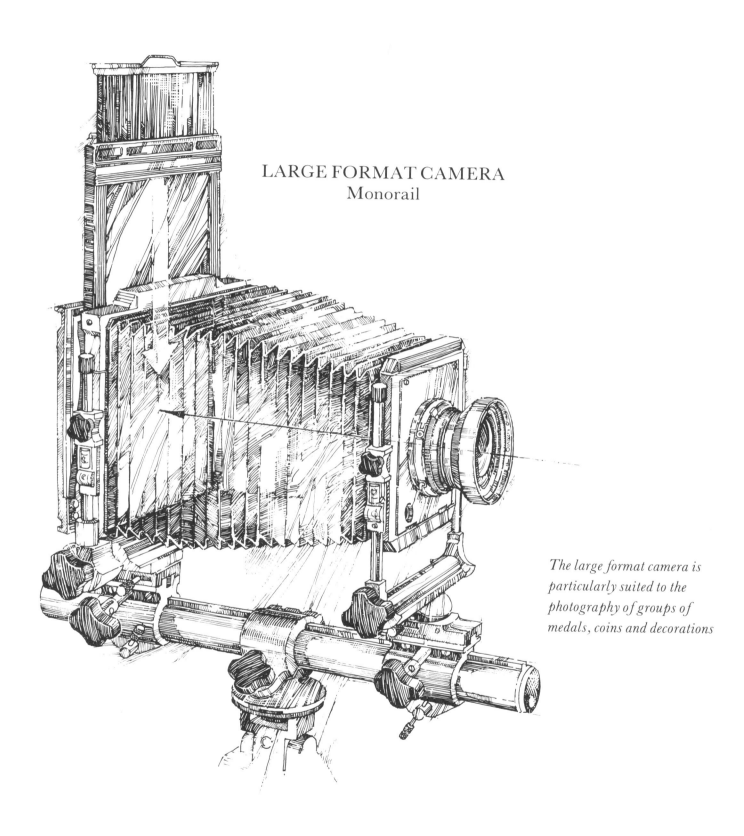

LARGE FORMAT CAMERA
Monorail

*The large format camera is
particularly suited to the
photography of groups of
medals, coins and decorations*

Photographic Equipment
Initial outlay

Despite rivalry in the photographic industry and the introduction of new equipment and gadgets the basic principles have changed little. Most cameras in this highly competitive market are capable of producing excellent results, with variations that are often difficult to discern; efficient operation excepted. Expensive equipment is justified for professional use, but the additional cost is generally disproportionate to the superiority of the end result. There is no universally ideal camera. One should select a camera and accessories that are ideal for the specific application. The larger the film size, the greater the operating expense – usually, however, with some discernible merit in the result.

Choice of format

The question of format hinges on both the dimensions of the originals and the ultimate image size required. An individual photograph of each coin is essential if optimum lighting effects and exposure are to be achieved, due to variations of the fabric, patina and the peculiarities of coin types. Coins photographed individually are best accommodated within a square format, being closest to the shape of the coin. It is often preferable to view both the obverse and the reverse simultaneously. This may be done by joining negatives, prints or transparencies side by side to form an oblong format with the obverse and reverse to view. However, other than for projection, it is usually more convenient to do this during the reproduction stage.

Reproducing obverse and reverse to view in the camera

It is possible with a large format camera to juxtapose both obverse and reverse simultaneously on a single sheet of film in the camera. This is done by exposing half the sheet at a time, by withdrawing the slide only halfway during exposure, assisted by a guideline on both the viewing screen and the slide. The sheet of film is rotated through 180° in the slide holder, in a dark room, thereafter exposing the other half. By this technique individual treatment can be given to both obverse and reverse by varying both the lighting and exposure. The careful choice of a suitable background is important to this method and the use of black velvet is especially suitable for camouflaging any join, as it will reproduce a saturated black.

Instant print cameras are useful to numismatists for checking complex lighting schemes and some conventional cameras offer instant print accessories. Choice of format should be large enough to accommodate coins at a ratio of 1:1.

The visible grain structure of the film's emulsion should be minimised in numismatic photography to improve the reproduction of fine detail. The greater the enlargement, the higher the magnification of the grain. Numismatists often scrutinize photographs of coins through a magnifying glass but sometimes find fine detail lost to disturbing graininess. By choosing a format which accommodates coins at 1:1 or larger, grain can be minimised with the added bonus of better colour saturation and image sharpness. The 56 mm x 56 mm format is ideal, as it will accommodate most coins at 1:1 ratio. The economical and versatile 35 mm (24 mm x 36 mm) produces excellent results. However, it is not ideal because it is too small to accommodate the larger coins at a ratio of 1:1.

Degree of acceptable grain structure and sharpness

The advantages of 1:1 scale (often referred to as same size, or life size)

Where transparencies are to be used for projection, consideration should be given to the choice of the format and availability of projectors, especially in the case of itinerant lecturers wishing to make use of loan equipment.

Suitable format for visual aids

Having selected a format, a camera with the most suitable components and accessories should be considered.

The shutter is a mechanism which regulates the duration of the exposures. It usually incorporates a flash synchronization device.

Shutter

The iris diaphragm is a thin opaque disc usually comprised of a series of interleaving variable blades incorporated within the optical system. Its function is to vary the size of the aperture (f-stop) thus controlling the amount of light which reaches the film plane and altering the depth of field.

Variable iris diaphram

Certain of the more sophisticated shutters incorporate a mechanical ring, which once engaged presents a selection of proportional aperture/speed ratios. There are basically two types of shutters:

Aperture/speed coupling

The between-the-lens shutter (diaphragm type) is situated between the camera lens elements. It consists of an arrangement of interleaving blades, pivoted at their outer edges, enabling them to open outwards and present a clear aperture simultaneously. The mechanism is designed to minimise operating time, thereby making fast shutter speeds possible.

Between-the-lens shutter

The focal plane shutter, situated slightly in front of the focal plane, exposes a strip of picture area successively across the film plane through the use of one or two metal or rubberised cloth roller blinds, which permit a rapid sequential exposure over the full film frame.

Focal plane shutter

An electronic shutter (battery operated) has been introduced into both the between-the-lens and, more recently, the focal plane shutters. With the great strides in micro chip technology, certain electronic components have been substituted for mechanical ones, setting new standards of consistency and accuracy. However, the difference in image quality will not usually be discernible in prac-

Electronic shutter

tice from the results achieved with a good mechanical shutter.

Fully automatic shutters without manual override are not suitable for coin photography.

Single lens reflex (SLR) cameras with between-the-lens shutters usually incorporate an auxiliary shutter within the body of the camera. Its function is to exclude light during viewing and focusing when the between-the-lens shutter has to remain open to enable the operator to focus his image. *Single lens reflex auxiliary shutter*

Camera shutters have an M and an X flash synchronization selector. The M setting is used with flash bulbs because the shutter has to be delayed momentarily to coincide with the maximum flash output, which takes longer to reach its peak than the electronic flash when the X setting is used. *Flash synchronization*

Focusing devices are fundamental to all but the simplest camera and those with a fixed focus are not suitable for coin photography. *Focusing devices*

Meticulous care must be taken to ensure optimum focus. This should always be done at full aperture using a focusing magnifier. An area of fine detail, particularly in the case of coins struck in high relief, should be selected midway between the two extremes of the coin's depth, i.e. the eye of an effigy. A single direct modelling light positioned at a low angle is useful to determine critical focus. Having achieved correct focus in the centre of the viewing screen, it is important to ensure that this focus extends to the corners. In many circumstances the outer extremities of the coin's depth of field, particularly when the coin is positioned off-axis, will appear out of focus. Sharp focus over the whole field can be achieved by reducing the size of the aperture, i.e. *stopping down* through the full range, while visually assessing its effect on the depth of field. *Focusing* — *Control of depth of field and distortion by camera movements*

The various focusing devices and the cameras in which they are incorporated are summarized:

Positioning of the coin on an inclined plane (off-axis) possibly to achieve a desired lighting effect or to record details of an edge inscription will pose problems of focus and distortion. These can be eliminated by the use of a view camera with a swing back that brings the film plane parallel to the coin.

Large format camera

The larger format camera (technical view camera) usually varies in format from 172 mm x 232 mm to 84 mm x 115 mm. It generally consists of a rigidly mounted single rail, with variable front and back frames. The two frames are attached to a supple leather, light-tight bellows, and can be varied by means of rack and pinion, or friction drive mechanisms, to facilitate focusing. A lens is attached to the front frame by means of an interchangeable lens mount, and a ground glass viewing screen is fitted into the back frame, positioned at the film plane.

Sheet film holder

Having focused the image on the ground glass, a sheet film holder is then inserted between the spring-loaded ground glass and the back frame of the camera. This holder consists of a light-tight sheath with removable slide which fits snugly into the grooves of the sheath. It is hinged at one end, so that the film can be inserted easily. When the sheath has been loaded into the camera, the slide is completely withdrawn, presenting the unexposed film in position for exposure. After exposure, the slide is then replaced and the sheet film holder is removed.

A high degree of precision is called for in both the camera and the construction of the film holder; this camera has one of the oldest, most reliable and elementary methods of focusing. The image on the ground glass appears upside down in reverse and is free of parallax error at any focal length. It requires an inanimate subject (between focusing and exposure) and must be rigidly mounted and focused under cover of a dark cloth or focusing hood. However, these characteristics are not limiting to the coin photographer – most of the finest contemporary large format photographs of still-life subjects are taken by this method. Moreover, the technical view camera offers a series of mechanical adjustments, which allow the photographer to exploit all the optical possibilities of a lens. Additional mechanical adjustments on the camera provide optical manoeuvrability, such as swings, tilts, and rises and falls, not possible with other camera designs. These large format cameras come into their own when used for photography of complete coin sets, large medallions, medal groups, decorations and bank notes at a scale of 1:1.

The twin lens reflex system consists of a view-finder lens in addition to the camera lens. The image passes through the view-finder lens (usually with a large fixed aperture) and reflects on to a ground glass screen, via a rigid 45° angled mirror – reflecting the image the right way up, but in reverse. The actual camera system is situated below the view-finder lens. Both lenses are fixed to a common mount and focusing mechanism, in order to focus simultaneously. This system is not ideal for coin photography due to limitations of lens interchangeability, the additional optics required and the problem of parallax error which causes the view-finder image and the picture on the film to differ. Parallax error occurs due to the relative positions of the lenses and the consequent lateral differential of their optical axes. This error is greatly magnified at close range.

Twin lens reflex

Parallax error

The single lens reflex (SLR) eliminates the necessity for cumbersome twin lenses and their inherent problems. Both focusing and exposure are effected through a common lens. The 45° angled mirror is swung up momentarily before the shutter is released, thus allowing exposure of the subject on the film. It then returns to its former position. This instant return mirror is basic to most modern cameras in the 35 mm,

Single lens reflex (SLR)

311

60 x 60 mm and 60 x 70 mm formats. One drawback of this system – image illumination whilst working with small apertures – has been overcome by the introduction of the preset iris diaphragm. This iris remains at full aperture and only stops down to the preset aperture just before the shutter is released, immediately prior to the exposure being affected. The iris may be stopped down in order to assess the depth of field by depressing an overriding control. In addition, the overall image brightness is improved through the use of a Fresnel lens – a fluted lightweight plastic screen placed on the ground glass viewer, which deflects the light rays at the edge of the field towards the eye.

A pentaprism is incorporated into the focusing device of the SLR with eye level viewing and presents an upright image, the right way round. A variety of both fixed and interchangeable focusing screens is available. The screens usually consist of a ground glass viewer, sometimes with the addition of a Fresnel lens, to ensure its even illumination over the entire image field. Various centrally placed optical devices are incorporated in the screens to facilitate focusing.

The split image bi-prism screen is a focusing device which is comprised of two similar glass wedges centrally positioned in a ground glass screen. The centre line of the bi-prism is positioned in the focal plane. The forward or backward deviation from the focal plane causes the light rays to be deflected by the opposing prism faces, splitting the image laterally. When the camera is focused the images will merge into an unbroken line. This method is best suited to subjects

SLR with pentaprism

Interchangeable focusing screens

Split image bi-prism

with vertical lines and focusing may prove difficult with random subjects.

The ground glass screen combined with a Fresnel lens and a central microprism screen is particularly well suited to macro-photography which requires the focusing of intricate objects devoid of prominent lines or structures. The microprism screen is made up of a series of microprisms, based on a similar principle to the split image screen though it contains some 200 microprisms per square millimetre. When focused, a sharp, clear and bright image is presented. This screen is used in most SLR cameras. Many camera systems offer a variety of interchangeable focusing screens including combination screens. *Microprism screen*

Extension tubes/rings provide an elementary means of expanding the magnification range of a lens by increasing the lens-to-film plane distance. The rings usually consist of a series of hollow tubes of varying lengths with a lens and camera mount at opposite ends. They are fitted between the lens and camera body and may be coupled together in series. Some camera systems provide full camera automation, with macro-accessories, through a system of interconnecting coupling mechanisms which allow the photographer to exploit all the innovations of the camera. *Extension tubes/rings*

The bellows extension is similar in principle to the extension tube but has the advantage of being variable over a continuous range. The bellows extension is constructed of supple leather, in a concertina form, attached to front and back mounts with adjustable riders on two rails. One is for varying the lens-to-film plane distance (the degree of magnification), while the other is for altering the position of the complete system in order to focus without altering the degree of magnification. Some bellows extensions provide the added versatility of perspective correction, i.e. lateral shifts, swings, and tilts. *Bellows extension*

Macro-adapter rings are available in certain camera sys- *Macro-adapter rings* tems which permit lenses to be fitted in reverse, thereby enabling them to cover the macro range. These adaptations can yield good results at a nominal extra cost. However, the macro-lens is purpose built to give optimum results.

Lens shades/hood

A lens shade/hood is an important accessory which prevents extraneous light outside the subject area from entering the lens. Transverse reflection is inclined to occur between the lens elements and may cause flare, ghosting, or degradation of image contrast. The lens shade consists of a matt black open ended tube or collapsible rubber shade with a metal lens mount at one end, or the versatile adjustable bellow lens shade. For optimum effect, a lens shade should limit the cone of light to the area covered by the angle of view of the lens. This is achieved by increasing the length of the lens shade in relation to the diminishing angle of view (in proportion to the focal length). Care should be taken to ensure that the lens shade is the correct size. If it is too long, or narrower than the angle of view of the lens, it will result in vignetting (cut-off), i.e. a partial masking of the format. The lens shade is useful in protecting the lens from accidental abrasions and should be left permanently attached to the lens whenever practicable.

Tripod/
copy stand/enlarger

An adjustable device capable of holding the camera and its accessories free from vibration and parallel to the subject, with minimum obstruction, is an essential part of the coin photographer's equipment. There are several alternatives:

1. A sturdy tripod may be used with its removable centre column inverted and fitted with either a ball and socket or pan-tilt head, which enables the camera to be adjusted downwards parallel to the coin.
2. A special purpose copy stand is ideal. This usually consists of a heavy metal base plate with a vibration-absorbing mat, adjustable feet and a sturdy vertical column. The column usually has an adjustable rider and locking nut, with or without counterweights, or rack and pinion gearing.

3. Some manufacturers of enlargers offer camera conversions as accessories. The old base plate and column of a sturdy enlarger makes an ideal copy stand.
4. Professional studios are often equipped with extra heavy-duty, centre-column camera stands on castors with locking brakes. These stands, principally designed to accommodate large format cameras, may be used for coin photography.

A spirit level is essential to check the horizontality of the film, lens, and image planes. *Spirit level*

The cable release is an indispensable aid to vibration-free exposures at slow shutter speeds. A cable length of about 30 cm should prove practical for this application. It is convenient to use a cable release even at fast shutter speeds with electronic flash. *Cable release*

A double cable release consists of a double cable of two different lengths attached to a common plunger. One cable is attached to the camera release button and the other to the lens shutter release, via a thread housed in the front section of the bellows extension. In addition to its obvious function, it is used to synchronize camera lens and bellows operation. The bellows extension of certain camera systems are now automatically coupled to the lens and camera obviating the need for this accessory. *Double cable release*

Coin photography should be carried out in a clean, dust-free environment as dust, hairs, fluff, etc., have a tendency to settle on both the coin and the background. Normal brushing or wiping tends to cause a static electrical charge which results in the dust clinging tenaciously to surfaces, and is particularly noticeable at a scale of 1:1. Several cleaning aids are available from camera dealers such as a large blower brush (consisting of a large rubber bulb with an anti-static brush), anti-static cloth, chamois leather, or an aerosol can of compressed air. When dusting numismatic specimens extreme care must be taken not to mark or damage surface patina. *Problems of dust and static*

315

Lens surfaces should be kept free of dust, finger prints, etc., and are best cleaned by removing dust with the blower brush or compressed air, then lightly cleaning their external surfaces with an anti-static cloth or chamois leather. In severe cases, such as stubborn finger prints or greasy marks, anti-static lens cleaning fluid may be used sparingly.

A camera designed to accommodate interchangeable lenses and optical accessories is an essential prerequisite for the photography of coins. One carefully selected lens and appropriate optical accessories are all that is required.

Consider the early camera obscura (a dark enclosure with a small hole in one wall). Its small aperture will admit a narrow band of converging light rays portraying the overall scene, immediately outside it, on to the opposite inside wall. Light rays from different areas of the scene pass through the aperture at various angles but do not intermingle, thus forming an image (upside down, reversed left to right). The camera obscura by virtue of its small aperture may produce an unsharp image through refraction of light at the point of entry. Conversely, a large aperture will cause the light rays to scatter, also producing an unsharp image. Moreover due to the absence of image control, one has to contend with a fixed image perspective. To overcome these limitations, various optical contrivances were introduced such as the camera lucida of Dr. Robert Hook in 1668 and the true camera lucida of Dr. William Hyde Wollaston in 1807 who also invented the meniscus lens.

The photographic lens is a curved transparent glass/plastic disc or a series of various curved and/or plane glass/plastic elements, mounted as a unit through which an image is viewed. The principal function of a lens is to vary perspective and to reduce exposure time. The design of the lens is computed to refract the light rays passing through it, in a predetermined manner on the film, causing them to converge and projecting a sharply focused image.

Lens design and manufacture is complex, demanding highly specialised skills. Each application of a lens presents its own special problems. An outline of the main considerations will be useful in augmenting understanding of a lens and a practical test using a test chart will assist in discerning its capabilities which depend on the following diverse factors:

Lenses

Lens interchangeability

Principal function of a lens

Lens design and manufacture

Resolution and resolving power

Resolution is the ability of a lens to define detail. The resolving power of a lens is the numerical measurement of this ability expressed in lines per millimetre. Resolution is influenced not only by the lens, but by the performance of the film, the contrast of the subject, the chemistry and accuracy of the process, and freedom from halation.

Definition

Definition is the comprehensive term denoting both the shadow edge gradient (the acuteness of the exchange from light to shadow) and the resolution.

Compound lenses

Convex and concave lenses

Camera lenses consisting of a series of glass elements are known as compound lenses. These are cemented together in various combinations – either convex lenses which cause the light rays to converge, known as converging or positive lenses, or concave lenses which cause the light rays to diverge, known as diverging or negative lenses. In addition, air space left between elements may have an optical function. Convex lenses, by the convergence of light to a focal point, project a real image at a fixed distance behind the lens. Conversely, the concave lens, by causing the light rays to diverge, transmits the rays of light in a scattered form, which cannot be brought to a point of common focus. This phenomenon is known as a virtual image, i.e. the focal point is merely apparent, and appears to come from a point in front of the lens.

Focal length of a lens

The focal length of a lens is the distance between the centre and the focus. The focal length governs both the distance between the lens and and the subject, and the distance between the lens and the film plane. The longer the focal length of a lens, the larger the magnification of the image, the narrower the angle of view, and the greater the working distance between the subject and the camera. For numismatic photography it is desirable to have a reasonable working distance between the lens and the coin, to allow the unrestricted use of lighting and accessories. A lens of medium focal length will meet this requirement.

Use of a short focal length lens for coin photography should be avoided, as a foreshortened perspective on a close coin-to-lens distance may cause image distortion, which, though not always obviously apparent, is undesirable.

The angle of view of a lens is determined by its focal length and the diagonal of the format. The standard lens, e.g. 80 mm (56 mm x 56 mm format) or 50 mm (36 mm x 36 mm format) corresponds approximately to the human eye.

The eye, however, constantly scans a fraction of its range, seeing only a small area in sharp focus at a time, but it has the ability to transmit an overall image to the brain. It does this automatically by focusing instantaneously on objects both near and far, without conscious effort, covering a wide angle of view and depth of field. The camera can be used to simulate this versatility through the use of interchangeable lenses, or a variable lens.

For coin photography a bellows extension and/or extension tube(s) are essential to obtain focus at a ratio of 1:1.

Significance of depth of field

Depth of field is the zone of acceptable focus on either side of an area of sharp focus. As the magnification increases the depth of field decreases. The special lenses designed for macrophotography, are computed to give maximum depth of field under high magnification, and have an extended range of small aperture settings.

Lens aberrations

Lens aberrations are the result of imperfections in an optical system, which prevent the convergence of light rays passing through at the principal point of focus.

The important task of the lens designer is to eliminate, or at least minimise, the several aberrations inherent in all optical systems. Aberrations which affect the image point on the axis of a lens are known as "axial aberrations". These are subdivided into spherical and chromatic aberrations and affect the entire field covered by the lens.

Spherical aberrations

A spherical aberration is the blurred effect caused when the light rays pass through a converging lens forming several

319

focal points simultaneously on different planes, preventing a common point of focus being reached. The rays furthest from the axis converge more acutely than the rays on the axis (due to the curvature of the lens).

Chromatic aberrations   A chromatic aberration is the effect caused by the difference in the degree of refraction of the components of light. White light consists of all the colours of the spectrum, as can be observed in the rainbow effect of white light which has been separated by a prism, e.g. the blue band of light is refracted more acutely than the red. With the refraction of light rays passing through a simple lens, the various colours may be similarly separated; each with its own degree of refraction. The result is that the individual wavelengths of colour have their own point of focus (focal length) on various optical planes and are thus not able to reach the common focal point.

Coma   Coma is the effect caused by the oblique refraction of light rays through an uncorrected lens. This has a tendency to produce off-axis focal points, as asymmetrical comet-shaped patches.

Astigmatism   Astigmatism is the effect caused by an off-axial aberration, due to structural defects in an optical system which prevent light rays from being brought to a point of common focus. An astigmatic lens precludes the simultaneous focusing of the vertical and horizontal rays of an image, due to the difference in their angle of incidence. Hence, the difference in the angle of reflection of the horizontal and vertical light rays which pass through the optical system. This effect prevents the overall field from being brought into sharp focus, allowing at best a compromise focus approximately midway between the two focal points.

Curvature of field   Curvature of field may occur when a subject is reproduced on to a flat film plane through a curved lens. The degree of this aberration escalates with the curvature-to-axis distance of the lens. The problem is not influenced by the aperture of the lens.

320

In addition to the principal aberrations, there are several other factors governing the quality of the lens:

Image distortion is the result of the variation in the magnification of an image, between the axial and off-axial portion of a lens. This variation causes the geometry of the image to differ from that of the original subject. Image distortion appears as either barrel distortion (the effect when the sides of a rectangle curve outwards) or pin cushion distortion (the effect when the sides of a rectangle curve inwards). Definition of the image is not affected by these distortions. *Image distortion*

The equality of illumination is the ability of a lens to transmit light rays with even distribution on the film plane. *Equality of illumination* The undesirable effects of uneven illumination can best be appreciated by observing the results of an incorrect condenser and/or adjustments being used in the optical system of an enlarger.

Vignetting is the loss, or reduction, of light at the edge of a lens, due to a lens shade of incorrect size, or other obstruction *Vignetting* in the path of a lens. It is on occasion deliberately introduced for effect, especially in portraiture, through the use of a vignetting mask, usually a card with a hole in it centrally positioned in front of the lens, to create a blank background to an image, with an edge of confused definition.

Within the interior of the lens, the reflections from the various lens elements tend to oscillate, causing an overall reduction of image contrast and detail; a light loss of about four *Internal reflection* percent usually occurs due to reflection at each glass/air boundary of a multi-element lens.

Most modern lenses of quality are multi-coated. A colour corrected coating is applied to the surfaces of the lens to reduce reflections, flare and ghosting, enhancing image detail *Lens coatings* and increasing brightness.

Flare is the unwanted effect on an image caused by multiple reflections from the glass surfaces or components of the *Flare* lens.

Ghosts

Ghosts are flare in the form of a defined image (usually distorted), such as the reflection of a window frame, or the outline of a lens diaphragm. These inverted images appear due to the transcurrent reflections between the various surfaces of the lens elements. This is often brought about by a direct brilliant light source in the field of view – such as a photograph taken facing the sun.

Circles of confusion

Circles of confusion are out-of-focus discs of light apparent in front of and/or behind the actual point of focus.

Diffraction

Diffraction takes place when light rays are deflected off an opaque edge (such as a lens diaphragm) thereby generating a new beam of light in a different direction, giving the appearance that the light has been bent around the opaque edge of the lens diaphragm. This phenomenon produces airy discs, an effect similar to circles of confusion but with the inclusion of dark and light concentric rings, formed when the light rays pass through the circular aperture. This adversely affects the resolving power of the lens.

Variable focus lens

The variable focus lens, a compound lens, is arranged in the lens barrel so that its focal length can be varied mechanically. This system requires re-focusing after each focal length variation.

Zoom lens

Zoom lenses, similar to variable focus lenses, are designed to maintain focus automatically. In addition, certain zoom lenses incorporate useful built in macro-optics and an extension tube.

Supplementary lenses

The supplementary (auxiliary) close-up lens is a simple, low-powered positive lens which is attached to the front end of a camera lens in the same way as a filter. Its function is to reduce the focal length of the camera lens thus reducing the corresponding lens-to-subject distance and increasing the scale of magnification. These lenses are usually obtainable in sets of varying strengths, e.g. 0,5 – 1,0 – 2,0 diopters – a diopter being the refractive power of a lens with the focal distance of one metre.

Though convenient and inexpensive their use should be confined to moderate magnification as inherent aberrations, particularly when used in multiples, cause image degradation. Practical exposure is not affected.

In addition to the excellent universal lenses there are special lenses designed to give optimum results in the macro-range and they are recommended for coin photography.

Specially designed macro-lenses

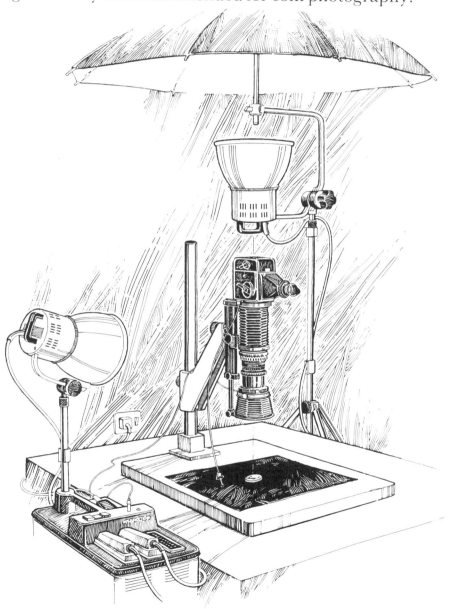

Photographic set-up for Axial illumination — see Page 341

323

Lighting

Light

Light is a form of electro-magnetic radiation which does not require any material conductor. Its velocity in a vacuum is 3×10^8 metres per second (186 000 miles per second). The eye has a limited capacity to perceive this transmission of energy by wave motion. The range of this capacity is referred to as the visual spectrum. Light waves travel at various lengths which are measured from crest to crest, i.e. wavelength. The visual spectrum ranges from approximately 400 nm to 700 nm. White light is an admixture of wave-lengths in a progressive series according to their refrangibility. This is evident from the visual spectrum (rainbow effect) which is produced when white light is passed through a prism. For convenience, only the primary colours of the visual spectrum are commonly referred to in the photographic context. They are blue, green and red. However, most film emulsions are sensitive to the whole visual spectrum including certain invisible rays, ultra-violet and infra-red.

Natural daylight

Natural daylight usually shows coins to best advantage and when simulated for coin photography excellent results can be achieved. However, complex factors govern its quality and intensity. The colour of daylight constantly varies due to the sun's relative position (redder at sunrise and sunset). Other environmental influences such as moisture content in the atmosphere, relative altitude, ultra-violet radiation and pollution may cause colour casts. The degree of diffusion may vary due to a change in the cloud formation. Moreover, insufficient light and restriction to peak daylight hours are

Artificial light

limiting. Consistent results may be achieved with an artificial light source. Through skilled operation it is possible to accentuate or diminish the apparent sharpness, enhance the toning of a coin, control or eliminate reflection and predetermine lighting quality and colour temperature.

Colour temperature

The hue of a light source, often referred to as warm (towards red) low colour temperature, or cold (towards blue) high colour temperature, is expressed in degrees Kelvin (°K). Mean

324

daylight (a combination of sunlight and skylight) has a colour temperature of approximately 5 500 °K. The measurement of colour temperature is based on the comparison of the hue emitted from a given incandescent "black body" light source: e.g. sun, tungsten lamp, molten metal, etc., which varies according to its relative temperature (degrees centigrade). The Kelvin scale starts at absolute zero (-273 °C).

$n\,°K = n + 273\,°C$

e.g. a black body heated to 2 000 °C = 2 273 °K

Colour temperature is particularly significant in colour photography, and its understanding and application cannot be over-emphasized. To produce consistent and faithful colour reproduction, variations in the colour temperature of the light source should be minimised. It is essential to provide the correct colour balance for which the film emulsion is *Colour balance* designed. The capacity of the human eye to discern contrast range and hue is vast when compared to the limitations of colour film. The eye has the ability to disregard colour casts caused by environmental influences so that the mind is not conscious of them. With the absence of psychological interpretation, colour film demands an accurate colour temperature and the exclusion of environmental colour casts, if faithful colour reproduction is to be achieved.

Coin photography calls for a high degree of light output due to the necessity to stop down to a small aperture to cover the shallow depth of field. Adequate capacity is required to bounce, diffuse, or redirect light to achieve the desired effect, and to counter the fall off in light intensity due to the use of extension tubes, bellows, or bellows extension required to obtain focus at the ratio of 1:1.

325

The increase in exposure may be determined by the following equation:

$$\text{Effective f-stop} = \frac{\text{Indicated f-stop x lens-to-film plane distance}}{\text{focal length}}$$

The effective increase in exposure required is calibrated on certain bellows extensions. This factor may also be simply determined through the use of a chart designed to indicate the bellows factor.

Inverse square law The intensity of illumination is inversely proportional to the square of the light-source-to-subject distance: e.g. a light source covering an area at a distance of one metre covers four times the area at a distance of two metres. Therefore, if the light-source-to-subject distance is doubled the intensity of illumination is reduced to one quarter.

In such areas the effective f-stop (aperture size) differs from its calibration on the aperture setting ring due to the effective fall off of light brought about by this extension. The calibration of the aperture setting ring only applies to the fixed lens-to-film plane distance.

The use of very fast film emulsions (high sensitivity to light) does not present a practical alternative to artificial light because the inevitably coarser grain of a high speed film is not conducive to fine detail at high magnification. Conversely, the extended exposure times of medium to slow speed films may produce colour imbalance caused by reciprocity failure between the colour layers of the emulsion (this is dealt with in the chapter on film). Films designed for exposure longer than 1/10th of a second can present a problem of camera shake. Even when mounted on a rigid tripod at a 1:1 ratio the slightest movement or vibration is greatly magnified. Although excellent results can be achieved with natural daylight, particularly with black and white film, constant results *Advantages of artificial* of quality especially in colour are best obtained with artificial
light

light, ideally with electronic flash. A large variety of lighting equipment is available.

Ordinary domestic lamps of incandescent tungsten filament type, due to their small light flux and low colour temperature, are unsuitable for coin photography.

Photo flood lamps are suitable due to greater light intensity. They are relatively inexpensive but have several drawbacks, such as a comparatively short working life and a variation in colour temperature with age (towards red), due to the tungsten deposits which build up inside the bulb. They are susceptible to premature failure if angled in certain positions and are particularly sensitive to shock. They emit great heat and need to be used in a lamp housing with effective heat dissipation and are prone to premature failure if subjected to an unstabilised surge in mains voltage. *Photo flood lamps*

Tungsten halogen quartz iodine lamps have a high intensity relative to their small size, a constant colour temperature, long life and heat resistance. Tungsten halogen bulbs must be kept on a horizontal plane during operation and are very sensitive to shock. They may not be touched to the extent that no direct skin contact may be made with the tube (i.e. during insertion). The high operating temperature of tungsten halogen lamps is uncomfortable when working at close range and the quality of light is usually too harsh for direct application. *Tungsten halogen lamps*

Fluorescent lamps are economical and emit little heat. These luminescent light sources function by exciting fluorescent film within a closed tube and they are not recommended for coin photography in colour, while for black and white, they are artistically limiting. *Fluorescent lamps*

The modern version of the old eyebrow-singeing powder flash consists of magnesium ribbon in an oxygen filled glass bulb, with a shatter proof coating, screw base and terminals. Bulbs are triggered either singly or in multiples, synchronised to the camera shutter. They yield the highest light intensity *Expendable flash bulbs*

327

for the lowest capital outlay but are the most expensive to operate as they are expendable and time consuming. They are unsuitable for the photography of coins as they do not provide a preview of the lighting effect and require the use of auxiliary modelling lights, or instant prints for reference.

Small portable flash units

Small portable flash units, powered by wet cells, nickel cadmium or alkaline batteries, usually do not have sufficient power for creative coin photography because they have limited capacity which affords only harsh direct lighting or a shallow depth of field. Moreover, they do not incorporate the necessary modelling lights.

Electronic flash

The ideal light source for colour photography of coins is an electronic flash system consisting of a power pack with a capacity of approximately 1 500 joules, two lamps with built-in modelling lights, and the appropriate accessories. This system requires the greatest capital outlay but the running costs are neglibible and the advantages are:

Advantges

1. The high light output enables photographs to be taken with diffused or bounced light at the smallest lens aperture affording greater depth of field and artistic scope.
2. Consistent colour temperature is maintained by a built-in voltage stabiliser.
3. Camera shake and vibration are eliminated because the extremely short flash duration effectively freezes movement.
4. Superior apparent sharpness is obtained.
5. Operator discomfort is minimised. When working at close quarters for long periods with lights that emit great heat the operator is subjected to considerable discomfort. In the case of electronic flash, the great light intensity is for such short duration that no operating discomfort is experienced and the modelling lights need only to be switched on for short intermittent periods.
6. Slow speed films with their inherently finer granularity and superior image quality can be used.
7. Reciprocity failure between the layers of film emulsions

328

(due to excessively long exposure which results in colour *Basic principles of* distortion) is eliminated. *operation*

8. Running costs are low – flash tubes usually last for thousands of flashes and a robust unit is virtually trouble free.

An electronic flash is produced by passing a high voltage current via a capacitor through a special robust glass or quartz tube, usually filled with xenon, krypton and small quantities of other rare inert gases, selected to produce the correct colour temperature, and sealed at each end with an electrode. As a result of the high voltage the gas is ionised, made electrically conductive, and an intense luminous charge flashes across to the opposite electrode. A third electrode coiled around the outside of the flash tube is often incorporated. With rapid advances in electronic technology, capacitors have become lightweight and compact. They are powered by a direct mains input, incorporated in a power pack with carrying handle and control panel, and have a bank of input sockets for individual lamp head leads. Alternatively, small capacitors are housed individually in the lamp heads each incorporating separate control panels. They are synchronised through interconnecting cables, slave units (photo-electric cells), or cordless infra-red triggering devices.

The control panel of the electronic flash usually consists *Controls* of:

a) mains on/off switch
b) audio visual recycling indicator
c) modelling light on/off switch
d) power and modelling light distribution selector
e) input sockets for synchronisation lead, lamp head leads and electronic exposure meter
f) auxiliary triggering devices – i.e. slave units, infra-red, etc.
g) fuse panel.

Lamp heads are usually comprised of a flash tube with a *Lamp heads* central modelling lamp, such as quartz iodine or photoflood, in an adjustable housing which allows variations in focus from flood (wide beam with lower intensity) to spot (narrow beam with higher intensity). They incorporate interchangeable reflectors, a carrying handle, individual fuses and accessory mounts, and are attached to an adjustable stand. Stands should be sturdy, lightweight, easily adjustable to below table top height, and reasonably portable.

Light meters The function of a light meter is to measure light intensity accurately and to convert the measurement into a range of practical camera settings related to the emulsion sensitivity (speed) of the film, i.e. ISO (ASA/DIN).*

Various light meters are available either incorporated within the camera or as a separate instrument. Despite the sensitivity and sophistication of these instruments one should bear in mind that they are only a means to an end and optimum results still require subjective human discernment. However, an exposure meter brings the photographer within optimum range and should be regarded as a useful tool, especially in the numismatic context, where very accurate exposures are required and extreme variations in the reflective index of metallic surfaces, textures and finishes are often encountered on a single specimen. Ideally, the objective is to reproduce the full tonal range and, in the case of colour, the subtle hues of the coin's patina. This is achieved by the correct combination of lighting, exposure and processing. Any minute degree of under- or over-exposure will cause the visual highlight or shadow areas of the range to merge and the quality of the picture to suffer. This is not usually obvious, within reasonable tolerances, other than by visual comparison with the ideal result. When photographing coins it is necessary to bracket exposures. This is done by establishing the correct exposure using a meter, and exposing four additional frames at half f-stop intervals on either side of the theoretically correct exposure. In cases of great variation in the surface of a coin, bracketing may have to be extended. The inclusion of a small density chart (grey scale) on the

*See page 343

photograph or an adjacent film frame will assist in evaluating the ideal exposure. The optimum exposure should be selected by careful scrutiny of the film on a light table or backlit diffuser. Instant prints are not usually practical for this critical determination. The extravagant use of film is a relatively small price to pay towards achieving perfection.

Selenium cell meters incorporate a photo resistor cell which changes the resistance of the current passing through it when exposed to light. This resistance is recorded on a micro-ammeter and the resultant light intensity measurement is then converted by means of a calibrated scale to practical camera settings. It does not require batteries and is inexpensive though relatively insensitive. *Selenium cell meters*

Cadmium sulphide (CDS) meters have a far greater sensitivity than selenium cell meters and are comprised of a photo-resistor, small alkaline battery and micro-ammeter. The electrical resistance of the cadmium sulphide cell changes with the intensity of the light and is recorded by a galvanometer in the circuit. *Cadmium sulphide (CDS) meters*

Silicon photo cell meters have an even greater sensitivity. *Silicon photo cell meters*

Meters are incorporated in most modern 35 mm cameras and usually record the exposure calculated by a photo cell behind the lens. They are useful for any photography not involving the use of flash. They automatically compensate for the fall-off in light reaching the film due to bellows extensions, lens aperture variations and filter factors, only recording the actual light about to affect the exposure. As these meters are primarily intended to record exposures quickly and conveniently from the camera position, without close-up meter readings, their receptors are usually made more sensitive towards the centre assuming that most subjects are positioned in the centre of the format. *Meters incorporated within the camera*

However, the precise exposure required for the combination of a highly mirrored field and a grained effigy in the macro range, for example, could not be determined accurately. Built-in meters are generally automatically or semi-automatically coupled, either mechanically or electronically, to the setting of the aperture and speed of the camera. Fully automatic cameras without manual adjustment are not suitable for coin photography. Some modern large format cameras provide an exposure probe device or meter attachment that records both average and selective readings on the ground glass viewing screen. These spot readings are generally very accurate and automatically compensate for many variable factors, i.e. increased exposure required in relation to the bellows extension, filter factors, etc.

There are basically two methods of taking a meter reading, the most common being to record the average intensity of light reflected from the subject towards the camera by taking the reading from a neutral grey card substituted for the coin. The other method is to record the intensity of the incident light on the subject by placing the meter on or next to it with its receptor, covered by a white translucent diffuser, towards the camera. The effect of the diffuser is to transmit a uniformly bright average incident light to the meter. Where practical a mean average between the two measurements should be taken to establish the more suitable exposure.

Electronic exposure meter

Conventional light meters cannot record an electronic flash of light, but a specially designed meter, which will not react to conventional light sources, is used. The meter is placed next to the coin and a flash is triggered which causes the needle to record the intensity of the flash and usually remains in that position for approximately a minute. The incident light value indicated is matched against a scale which gives the aperture setting. As in the case of conventional light meters the emulsion sensitivity ISO (ASA/DIN) must be set. The shutter speed is not indicated on this meter as the constancy and extremely short duration of the flash necessitates the selection of only one camera shutter speed. This shutter speed is stipulated by the camera manufacturer according to

332

the design of the shutter.

Automatic flash units usually incorporate a flash meter *Automatic flash* with a film speed setting, an aperture selector and a photo-electric cell. The flash is emitted at full power and its duration is determined by the intensity of light reaching the photo cell reflected from the subject. As with conventional flash, allowance should be made for bellows extension or filters.

The initial average exposure may be determined by *Ideal exposure without a meter* photographing a graduated density chart at each aperture setting. Evaluating the results are simplified by the inclusion of a small card bearing the selected aperture setting in each photograph. For convenience, the individual frames of this test film should not be cut after processing, as each frame must be compared to select the optimum exposure. This is determined by selecting the exposure which records all the density variation patches on the test chart faithfully. In the case of under- or over-exposure the frames will merge at either end of the scale.

A colour temperature meter records the colour tempera- *Colour temperature meter* ture of light and, if necessary, indicates the light balancing filter required to obtain the colour temperature for which the film was designed. For coin photography it is preferable to avoid the use of light balancing filters by choosing an artificial light source with a constant colour temperature.

When an object is illuminated a shadow is cast. This is *Shadows* simply the area shielded from illumination by the intervening object and is inseparable from every lighting situation whether natural or artificial. A significant gift of creation, shadow forms an integral part of the earth's day/night scheme. Its phases produce a variety of shapes, sizes and intensities which enhance, beautify and dramatise this magnificent world, shielding it in part from direct sunlight. Shadow gives apparent shape and form to everything around us and is a constituent part of nature's vast capacity to present the visual spectrum in an infinite variety of shades, colours and moods, which the photographer should try to emulate. The size, shape, tone and apparent sharpness of a shadow is determined by the intensity of the light source, its effective coverage, relative distance and position from the intervening object, the object's size and shape, and the surface on which the shadow is cast. A naked point source of light (i.e. without a reflector) will produce a sharp shadow, when intercepted by an opaque object, irrespective of the relative distance between the light source, object and background – the nearer the object and point of light the larger the shadow cast. The nearer the background to the object the smaller and harsher the shadow cast. Shadows thus produced are generally of even intensity.

When a reflector is introduced the resultant shadow cast by an intervening object has a dark core called the umbra surrounded by a lighter area of diffused shadow referred to as the penumbra.

Reflectors Reflectors are available in numerous shapes, sizes and designs, and in choosing the most suitable type for the application their principal functions should be borne in mind. They are:

1. To intercept and redirect multi-directional light rays towards the subject.
2. To vary the light beam from flood to spot. The desired variation is usually achieved via a simple mechanism enabling the operator to adjust the relative bulb-to-reflector distance.

In coin photography the most important function of a reflector is its capacity to diffuse light and thereby simulate the varying qualities of natural daylight.

Reflectors are generally constructed of anodized aluminium which withstands high temperatures, is durable, lightweight and rust-free. The inner reflective surfaces are usually granulated to diffuse the light and soften the shadows. Reflectors may also be constructed of other materials able to withstand heat, and are often painted with a white heat-resistant colour corrected paint.

Mirrored reflectors will produce high light intensities with harsh contrast, ill-suited to coin photography particularly when colour film is used.

The effect of a reflector is governed by its shape, size, reflective index and relative position. A simple flat reflector is very useful for lighting the shadow near the subject and should form part of the photographer's lighting equipment. An inexpensive white cardboard sheet covered one side with crushed aluminium foil may be used. For highlighting the rim of a coin only, a piece of white paper or foil approximately four millimetres wide and twenty millimetres long can be used either as a straight, angled or circular reflector. While accentuating the rim, it minimises unwanted reflections on the surface of the coin which would in certain cases flatten its apparent depth.

Shapes

A spherical reflector produces a broad beam for general illumination.

Spherical reflectors

An elliptical reflector causes the rays to converge and concentrates the beam in a relatively small area, resulting in high contrast and intensity and is therefore not recommended.

Elliptical reflectors

A parabolic reflector (in theory) gives a parallel beam of light which is equal to the diameter of the reflector. The resultant quality of light is particularly suited to coin photography.

Parabolic reflectors

A light bank consists of a series of reflectors mounted in a frame to produce a diffused flood of light. Though suitable in the studio situation it is not easily portable.

Light banks

A flood reflector with a hemispherical cap consists of a large shallow dish with a centrally positioned hemispherical cap placed directly in front of the bulb and held in position by three springs. The function of the cap is to block the direct rays, thereby producing a diffused light. This reflector is suitable for the photography of coins.

Hemispherical cap reflector

Spill rings Spill rings are a series of concentric matt black rings similarly positioned to the hemispherical cap. Their function is to block the wide angled rays thus producing a well defined beam. Therefore they are not suitable for coin photography.

Ring light/flash A ring light/flash consists of a circular reflector and tube, or a circular bank of reflectors, positioned axially around the camera lens directly facing the subject, surrounding it with a shadowless even illumination. A useful device for photographers with a low budget, though artistically limiting, it may be used to good effect if the coin is carefully positioned slightly off-axis to improve the modelling. An auxiliary lamp may be used for setting up.

Umbrella reflectors The umbrella reflector was introduced in France in 1854 to soften the shadows of the newly invented arc lights. By 1899 Houghtons of London were selling canvas lined wicker basket reflectors. Their popularity dwindled with the transition to tungsten filament lamps but with the introduction of the electronic flash they gained popularity once more. The modern umbrella reflector is highly recommended for coin photography. The umbrella frame often has a reversible and detachable covering with a white reflective surface on one side, giving a very diffused soft lighting quality. On the other side is a silver granulated surface which gives a diffused light with slightly stronger shadows and is ideal for coin photography. Umbrella reflectors are about 1,20 metres in diameter yet lightweight and portable. They are positioned with the concave surface directly in front of the light source in order to intercept and redirect (bounce) the light.

Diffusers A diffuser is translucent material placed between a direct light source and the subject in order to diffuse the light and produce a hazy lighting quality. Diffusers are conveniently available as accessories (e.g. translucent umbrellas), or may be improvised with nylon or white silk stretched over a frame. A light tent diffuser is a cone made of translucent material, the apex of which surrounds the lens. Its effect may be con-

336

trolled by the thickness of the material and the relative position of the light source to the cone.

Barn doors (adjustable matt black metal shields) which are attached to reflectors to exclude sections of the light beam, and conical snoots to reduce light coverage and accentuate specific areas are not required for coin photography. *Lighting accessories*

Perhaps the most important consideration in producing a photograph of fine quality is the lighting. Through lighting technique the photographer is able to influence and control: *Applied lighting*
a) shape and form
b) texture
c) apparent sharpness
d) contrast
e) shadow
f) reflection
g) apparent dimension
h) colour
i) mood
j) emphasis
k) perspective.

Many photographers advocate set lighting schemes which incorporate diffusion chambers, 45 ° angled mirrors, prisms, etc. These can be effective and convenient but at best produce average results. The lighting of each coin demands individual attention and consideration should be given to:
a) the fabric of the coin
b) the pictorial content
c) condition (i.e. degree of wear)
d) reflective surfaces and their relative contrast
e) toning
f) colour
g) physical dimensions
h) edge inscriptions, decorations or special features
i) special requirements such as incuse or embossed strikings.

The overall lighting effect is strongly influenced by the

337

Background choice of background which should be chosen with circumspection. A busy background design in most cases distracts the viewer and vies with the coin for prominence. Texture (of cloth, etc.) is magnified when enlarged or projected and may appear quite different to that of its actual scale. Background colour and tone should be chosen to complement and enhance the coin rather than on the merits of its appearance. A judicious choice of background can greatly assist in the three dimensional quality and overall presentation of the coin. Consideration should also be given to final imposition: for example, a patchwork kaleidoscope of background colours or a range of half tones presented simultaneously in a publication or display can prove aesthetically disastrous. A coloured background, if used in a conventional way, will produce a colour cast as a result of its close proximity to the coin. The degree of colour cast is commensurate with the strength of the hue, the refractive index of the background and that of the coin, and the relative angle of incidence of the light. Though not always obvious to the untrained eye, casts do affect the colour balance of the photograph. Fine quality black velvet is suited to most coins and provides an excellent saturated black background which appears shadowless on film, irrespective of the lighting position. This is due to its capacity to absorb light and its inability to reflect it. In addition background flare is eliminated. Its fine texture is undetected at high magnification and black backgrounds are easily impositioned without unsightly joins for reproduction. Well lit black background paper will usually appear on film as murky grey and, if black velvet is not available, it is best to use black and white photographic paper which has been exposed and processed.

White card White card is a good alternative background, as it is neutral, eliminates colour casts, is complementary to many coins, is particularly suited to black and white coin photography and the requirements of auction catalogues, and is easily impositioned and deep etched.

Deep etching is a technique whereby individual photo- *Deep etching*
graphs are carefully separated from their backgrounds by
skilfully painting the area around the coin with an opaque
liquid. The coin may then be impositioned on a black,
coloured or white background. There are disadvantages to
this technique as deep etching is inherently prone to flare and
halation around the edges. Even though expertly executed it
is often obvious, especially on a hammered coin of irregular
circumference and depth which may have cracks, nicks and
other peculiarities which should be shown. Subtle, though
important, background shadows which sometimes enhance
three dimensional perspective are lost.

An alternative is to produce a mask which is often su- *Masking*
perior to hand blocking. This is simply a sheet of high contrast (line) film exposed in contact and register and superimposed as a background mask on the original. By this
method a variety of photographs can be produced on a continuous black or white background, either monotone, tinted or
in colour, with each specimen individually illuminated and
exposed to its best advantage, at the reproduction stage.

The ideal is to produce a photograph which does not require any background treatment.

In addition to the use of black velvet the coin may be
placed on a transparent colourless sheet of perspex, free from
scratches, used as a working surface and suspended by a
frame, clamps, blocks or other improvisation, level and parallel to the film plane. (Check with a spirit level.) The distance
between the perspex and the floor should be variable. By
placing the card or background material at various levels beneath the perspex one is able to control the degree of intensity
and shape of the shadows or to eliminate them. The rim
and/or edge of a coin may be illuminated effectively from below the perspex, thus reproducing it accurately and minimising reproduction costs. Moreover, the magnified texture of

the background can be controlled or eliminated by its relative position below the coin. Special out-of-focus background effects are made possible in this way, but should be used with circumspection.

Lighting the background The background beneath the perspex should be separately and evenly illuminated. This is achieved by placing two lamps equidistant from the background at an angle of 45°. Equality of illumination can be checked by placing a pencil or similar straight object on the centre of the background. The operator must remain well out of the path of the light, visually check that the shadows are even, of similar length and intensity, and, if necessary, adjust the relative position of the lights accordingly.

Coins vary from fragile, incuse, embossed wafer thin Bracteates to ancient Greek portraits struck in highest relief. Coins should not be treated as flat artwork, but their three dimensional qualities should be accentuated, showing, for example, thickness of flan or die cracks.

Lighting the coin The object should be to illuminate the coin with maximum visual impact, to reproduce it accurately, and to accentuate its beauty. One should endeavour to reproduce maximum gradation of tone and in the case of colour film to record its subtle hues. Moreover, one should strive to achieve sharpness, general colour balance and to co-ordinate apparent shape, form, texture and harmony. A common error is the tendency to over-illuminate coins. Photography, writing with light, is only half the equation; the other half, writing with shadow, is as important, for without light there is no visual image and without shadow there is no visual form. The skilful use of shadow by the great masters, such as Rembrandt, contributed immeasurably to the dramatic effect of their paintings.

It is preferable to commence setting up in a darkened room, with white walls, to eliminate any colour casts. Initially the axis of the coin should be horizontal and parallel

340

to both the lens and film plane. This should be checked with a spirit level or parallel mirror device. In seeking to emulate diffused natural daylight a single diffused light source of adequate intensity should be used. An electronic flash with modelling light and a silver granulated umbrella reflector is particularly suitable. The single light should be positioned as close to the lens axis as possible (without touching the camera or its accessories). The light source should be beamed towards the umbrella reflector away from the coin so that diffused light is redirected towards the coin. The angle may be slightly varied off-axis. This axial illumination makes an ideal principle light source because its relative position to the coin and film plane produce foreshortened shadows and a subtle moulding effect similar to the bright haze of an overcast noon sky. This lighting quality is conducive to recording the subtle toning of coins and minimises extreme variations in the reflective index often encountered when photographing metallic surfaces.*

Axial illumination

An alternative lighting scheme is to interpose a clear optical glass at a 45° angle between the lens and the coin. A laterally positioned light source is then directed at the angled glass which partially redirects the light downwards, illuminating the coin axially while simultaneously allowing the exposure to be made through the glass from above. However, this method produces a higher contrast than that of the umbrella reflector and introduces an additional glass surface into the optical path.

By positioning the coin slightly off-axis a variety of hues, tones and lighting effects can be achieved and the photographer is presented with endless artistic possibilities. The coin axis may be varied by using a simple base or frame covered with background material fitted to a tilt and clamp mechanism, such as a ball joint of a tripod head. Alternatively, plasticine or preferably non-hardening plastic putty can be used. A small block of putty or plasticine is positioned

*See page 323

under the background material beneath the coin (never use in direct contact with coins) and it can then be adjusted at the desired angle. One should vary the angle of the coin through 45° and study the effect through the viewing screen of the camera, in order to select the most aesthetically advantageous angle. The single light source used on its own or in conjunction with a reflector(s) will often suffice to obtain optimum results.

Lighting to accentuate texture

By accentuating texture and/or highlighting the edge of a coin a dramatic effect can be achieved and the accent is placed on the structure, detail, apparent sharpness and the three dimensional quality. These effects are best assessed for each individual coin surface by placing a single light source, at least half a metre distant, at an obliquely low angle above the subject and varying its position radially (or that of the coin). By switching off the principal light the effect of the auxiliary light source may be determined. If the auxiliary light is adjusted to a higher position the shadows are shortened and if it is lowered they are lengthened. The intensity of shadow is strengthened by placing the light(s) nearer to the coin and made less dense by placing it further away. A fill-in light source may be used to soften the shadows, but should only be used in special circumstances as it is likely to produce unnatural additional shadows and, due to the size of the coin,

Checking complex lighting schemes

the effect of this light on selective areas is very limited. An instant print accessory attachment or camera may be used for checking the effect of a complex lighting scheme.

There is a variety of films and the appropriate choice for the specific application is important. Photographic emulsions, applied to a glass plate (still used for scientific and technological applications where extreme dimensional stability is required), a gelatin based sheet, a roll film, or printing papers, consist of a suspension of light sensitive silver halides: i.e. silver chloride, silver bromide, or silver iodide evenly applied and uniformly light-sensitive. Gelatin (a colloid) keeps the silver halide particles dispersed, while being sufficiently permeable to allow effective penetration of the processing solution, and in dry conditions the emulsion remains stable for long periods. The spectral sensitivity of halides is limited and they absorb only certain wavelengths of light. By adding complex organic chemicals to the emulsion the sensitivity range is expanded to cover the visual spectrum. In the case of black and white this is known as panchromatic film, which is a prerequisite for general coin photography. When developed chemically the latent image is greatly amplified. The minute silver halide particles form clusters, creating a grain structure. The larger the original light sensitive crystals the greater the area exposed in a given time and, consequently, the greater its sensitivity (speed).

Films

High speed films are not ideal for coin photography as minute detail is required. The sensitivity of photographic materials to light (film speed) is usually expressed arithmetically in ASA (American Standards Association) and/or logarithmically in DIN (Deutsche Industrie Norm) and more recently in a combination of the two ISO (International Standards Organisation). ASA 100 or DIN 21 = ISO 100/21° and at least one of these standard measurements are quoted on all containers of light sensitive film. The higher the index, the greater the sensitivity of the emulsion to light. These numbers appear on light meters and other photographic equipment and any one of these measurement standards may be applied as they all provide a similar yardstick. The ideal

Measurements of film speed

range of film speeds for coin photography is generally between 25 and 64 ASA or 15 and 19 DIN.

Graininess Graininess is the granular pattern of minute density variations in an apparent uniformly dense area of a photographic emulsion. Its effect is more pronounced with enlargement, fast film emulsions, increased density (through over-exposure and/or over-development) and under the magnifying glass of the numismatist.

Granularity Granularity is measured by a microdensitometer and is expressed as diffuse RMS (Root Mean Square) granularity:
5 = microfine
6 and 7 = extremely fine
8 – 14 = very fine

These measurements are usually indicated on data sheets available from film manufacturers.

Resolving power The demands of numismatic photography require a film with a high resolving power. This measurement is expressed in lines per millimetre and is often classified for convenience as:
Ultra high = 630 or more lines per mm
Extremely high = 250 – 500 lines per mm
Very high = 160 – 200 lines per mm
High = 100 – 125 lines per mm
Medium = 63 – 80 lines per mm

Line film Line film is designed primarily to record fine line detail in high contrast black and white without any intermediate tones. Though unsuited to general coin photography it is most useful for reproducing line originals, such as the wood cuts and etched plates often found in old numismatic literature. When reversed by contact printing (i.e. negative/positive – positive/ negative) it may be used as a transparent overlay for the comparison of similar coins and their relative die positions.

Principles of the colour film process Colour films combine the basic principles of black and white film with the fact that an admixture of the primary colours will produce virtually any colour in the visual spectrum. When these additive primaries – blue, green and red – are presented in equal balanced proportions white light is produced. Conversely, the complementary colours (or negative subtractive primaries) – yellow, magenta and cyan – are produced by subtraction of varying amounts of the respective additive primaries from white light. Very strong primary colours in balanced proportions will produce black, while lesser amounts in balanced proportion will produce neutral grey, and various other combinations will produce almost any colour. This is simply demonstrated by viewing the three transparent primary colours in various combinations on a backlit diffuser, or three projectors simultaneously focused but overlapping each with a transparency of the respective primary colour. It is obviously impractical to take three identical photographs in each of the primary colours and to combine them in register to form one colour photograph. The integral tripack colour film method was devised to control the absorption of the primary colours within a single composite film. During exposure light reaches the blue sensitive layer first and records the blue component of the subject. The silver halides in all of the emulsion layers are blue sensitive and in order to prevent blue affecting the bottom layers a yellow filter coating of microfine silver is applied under the blue sensitive layer. The next layer is green sensitive only, absorbing the green light and transmitting the red light to the next layer which is red sensitive. By this method multi-coloured subjects are faithfully reproduced. The strength of the complementary colours is directly related to the degree of absorption of the corresponding primary colours during the original exposure, e.g. if the red sensitive layer absorbs a greater degree of red a correspondingly greater percentage of cyan is formed chemically to reproduce the original image colour accurately. The halides are then removed by a bleach-fix bath.

The antihalation backing on an emulsion prevents the *Antihalation backing*

345

light which has passed through the coloured layers from reflecting back.

Colour prints are produced by exposing a colour negative composed of the complementary colours – yellow, magenta and cyan – on similarly coated photographic paper. In order to achieve a correct colour balance on the final print, the precise degree of exposure and colour filtration to be introduced into the path of the light source of the enlarger is determined by the use of a colour densitometer (by transmission or reflective measurement) and/or by the use of practical test strips.

Negative/positive process

Colour negative film is used for:

Direct reversal transparencies/slides/ diapositives

a) colour prints
b) printed transparencies yielding large eye-catching illuminated displays.

Colour transparencies (slides, reversal films or diapositives) are best suited for:

a) photo mechanical reproduction (printing)
b) projection
c) duplicate and display transparencies on direct reversal materials.

Colour prints, printed transparencies and black and white negatives can all be produced from transparencies via an intermediate-negative (internegative) or colour prints and printed transparencies may be produced from direct reversal materials.

Processed transparencies are composed of a positive image formed of transparent dyes. This is achieved by incorporating the entire negative to positive process within a single emulsion. It usually consists of a black and white colour sensitized layer which initially records the latent image and is developed to produce the negative layer of the emulsion. This is then reversed chemically (or evenly exposed to white light). The unexposed light sensitive portion of the silver halides are then darkened to produce the positive image. The original exposure records blue, green and red (the pri-

346

mary colours) which are then transferred chemically during the next stage of the process to form the complementary colours of yellow, magenta and cyan.

The dye destruction process is used for reproducing prints *Dye destruction process* and transparencies directly from the original transparencies. An alternative method of achieving the correct proportion of the complementary colours is the dye destruction process whereby the film emulsion is coated during the manufacture with equal proportions of the three complementary colours. During processing a percentage of these dyes is destroyed in relation to the corresponding degree of primary colour reflected from the subject.

In choosing an ideal colour film the following should be *Choosing an ideal colour film* considered:

1. The choice of negative or positive film.
2. The correct colour temperature of the film appropriate to the light source.
3. The choice of negative film with the appropriate reciprocity characteristics, i.e. films specially designed for shutter speeds of shorter than 1/10th of a second (S type) and those designed for shutter speeds of 1/10th of a second or longer (L type). In the case of positive film these are designated A type and B type respectively.
4. The exposure latitude of the film, which is its ability to record extreme variations in contrast.
5. The choice of amateur or professional film. It is preferable to use a professional emulsion for coin photography as it is another step towards consistent results. From the time of manufacture film emulsion undergoes a gradual change. Film manufacturers therefore usually programme their film to reach its optimum maturity before the designated date of expiry under typical amateur conditions, i.e. widely varying storage temperatures and the exposure of the film over an extended period. Though characteristically similar to the normal amateur emulsions, profes-

347

sional films are manufactured near to the optimum colour balance and the effective speed rating of each film emulsion batch is individually and precisely designated. Professional film should be refrigerated at 10 °C or lower to freeze the emulsion at its optimum colour balance, contrast, etc. Before use, the film should be thawed at room temperature for at least four hours in its original packing to prevent condensation. In practice, the use of professional emulsions at normal room temperature for approximately two weeks will not cause any undesirable change to occur. However, in hot and humid conditions special precautions must be taken. Amateur films are designed to be stored at room temperature.

Professional film should be refrigerated

6. Whether the film can be conveniently and expertly processed locally and whether the process is suitable for the photographer to handle if desired.

A filter is an optically flat transparent disc or square of coloured glass often with an anti-reflection coating. Coloured gelatin squares or other materials are also available (sometimes sealed between optically flat glasses). It is mounted in front of the camera lens by means of a screw ring, bayonet coupling or a frame. It may be placed in the path of the light source instead of in front of the camera lens thus avoiding possible image distortion. The function of a filter is to absorb certain colours of the spectrum whilst transmitting others, to accentuate or minimise a portion of the spectrum. The use of camera filters in coin photography should be avoided in most cases, as they introduce either two, or (in the case of gelatin sandwiched between glass) six additional surfaces between the lens and the coin which can affect the optimum quality of a lens. Buckled, poorly mounted gelatin filters which lack parallelism or imperfect glass surfaces with dust, finger marks, and scratches, etc., although not always apparent, will impair sharpness, contrast and general lens performance. Filters should therefore only be used if absolutely necessary.

Filters used for black and white photography differ from those used for colour photography as they have a higher density. Polarising, ultra-violet or neutral density filters can be used for both. Although it is normally preferable to reproduce an accurate panchromatic facsimile of a coin, in special cases filters may be useful for improving tonal contrast. An ancient patinated green coin may be improved by introducing a red filter which will increase the image contrast generally, and will darken the green and blue tones, whilst lightening the red. Conversely, a green filter will lighten the green, darken the red and slightly darken the blue. The correct choice of filter will be determined by the actual colours of the patina.

Colour compensating filters used in colour photography have a relatively low density range from 0,05, which is virtually colourless, to about 0,9 and are usually confined to cyan, magenta and yellow. Their function is to compensate

Filters

Black and white contrast filters

Colour compensating (CC) filters

349

for minor variations in the colour balance of a light source and those inherent in certain film emulsion coatings.

Light balancing filters Light balancing filters are used to modify the colour temperature of light (which may be determined by a colour temperature meter) to that for which a film is designed. They are usually available in sets of six and each filter has a different density, three blue to raise the colour temperature and three red (amber) to lower the colour temperature. These filters are usually calibrated in decamireds – a alternative unit of colour temperature : i.e. 1 degree Kelvin (°K) divided into 1 000 000 = 1 mired x 10 = 1 decamired which presents a minimal visible shift. When an artificial light source with correct constant colour temperature is used these filters are not required. Where artificial light is used with daylight film, or *Conversion filters* vice versa, a specific light balancing filter, known as a conversion filter, is used : e.g. to convert the colour temperature of an artificial light film of approximately 3 200 °K to daylight approximately 5 600 °K, a weak red (conversion) filter of about 12 decamireds is used.

Haze and skylight filters Haze and skylight filters are widely used for general outdoor photography to reduce haze, i.e. light scattered by moisture vapour and dust particles in the air – consisting principally of ultra-violet and blue light – and as a means of protecting the surface of the lens. They are not recommended for numismatic photography and should be removed.

Polarising filters Polarising filters help to control reflections of non-metallic surfaces and colour saturation by transmitting light in one direction while blocking out the light in another direction thus polarising the light. The degree of polarisation is controlled by rotating the adjustable ring filter to vary its axis. In addition, where practical, polarising filters should be placed over the light source. These filters do not alter the colour balance and may be used for either black and white or colour film. Despite their metallic composition many numismatic specimens acquire minute non-metallic particles on their surfaces and the reflected light can often be polarised. However, the results may lack vitality and appear similiar to photographs of plaster casts. In almost all cases skilfully controlled reflections yield more natural and aesthetically pleasing results.

Neutral density (grey) filters reduce the transmission of light, enabling the photographer to work with larger apertures under very bright light. This situation is not normally encountered when photographing coins, but a neutral density filter may be required for highly reflective surfaces. *Neutral density filters*

All but palest filters require an increase in exposure to compensate for the effective loss of light. This increase is usually designated on the filter, i.e. 1 x (1 f-stop) 2 x (2 f-stop). However, filter factors are automatically taken into account by meters which record through the lens. *Filter factors*

Processing and Printing

Standards often less than ideal

Doing one's own processing and printing

Professional laboratories

Many people are either unable to distinguish good processing from bad or erroneously accredit poor results to their own incompetence. Accurate processing and printing of film is vital if good results are to be achieved and this obvious fact is often overlooked. Photographic dealers generally act as agents for commercial processing and printing houses which usually churn out vast quantities of photographs quickly, at very competitive prices, and the standard, by the very nature of this type of operation, is often less than ideal. Superior camera equipment, time and much effort is wasted because of inferior processing and printing. There are two remedies for these problems:

1. To do one's own processing and printing. With black and white film this is relatively inexpensive and artistically rewarding. However, in the case of colour processing and printing it is not normally recommended unless large quantities of film are processed and printed regularly. This is due to the limited life of diluted colour processing solutions, capital intensive equipment, time, darkroom space, and all the economic ramifications. Precision colour processing must be consistent and the temperature of certain chemical baths is critical to within half a degree centigrade. The pH factor (acid/alkaline) must be carefully monitored, the solutions replenished or replaced at prescribed intervals, the wash water filtered, the temperature controlled, and the film handled with extreme care.

2. To find a good professional processing laboratory if possible, to meet the management and/or staff of the laboratory and to stress the critical requirements of coin photography. One should, in addition, monitor results by photographing the test card supplied in this book on at least one frame of each batch of film handed in for processing. This test is only meaningful if the film has been correctly stored before and after exposure and exposed under ideal lighting conditions, average contrast, correct

352

colour temperature, etc. Laboratory managers will usually welcome constructive monitoring. Careful selection of a processing laboratory and the mutual co-operation between photographer and management cannot be overemphasised. Even the finest, well-managed laboratories unfortunately encounter problems from time to time, as do the most expert photographers, and if and when such problems arise it is imperative to seek the cause objectively. It is extremely unlikely that the fault will lie in the original manufacture of the film. However, poor storage of a film which has passed its expiry date can be responsible for colour imbalance. It is a good idea to purchase a quantity of film with a common emulsion batch number in order to minimise the variables. Ideally one should carry out a practical test in order to establish the characteristics of the emulsion batch. The pre-exposed black edges of the film should be checked to ensure saturation. If the pre-exposed frame numbers and manufacturers markings appear abnormal it can reasonably be concluded that the processing is at fault. The test chart with its colour patches, density scale and black and white areas assists in recognising faults.

The most competent professional photographers have experienced the displeasure of producing a superb photograph only to see it shoddily reproduced in print. The quality of many fine originals is ruined during reproduction by one or more of the following:

Following through

a) the use of cheap unsuitable paper
b) inaccurate colour
c) incorrect density
d) incorrect contrast
e) incorrect register of the colour separations
f) being out of focus

The printer's proofs should be evaluated by the photographer, the total operation from concept to the final printed page should be monitored carefully at each stage, regarded as a team effort and the craftsmen involved should be acknowledged and encouraged.

Jungwirth, H. Leopold I – Karl VI, 1657-1740. Nach dem Werk [von] V. Miller zu Aichholz, A. Loehr, E. Holzmair: Österreichische Münzpragungen 1519-1938. Wien: Kunst-historisches Museum, 1975 (*Corpus nummorum Austriacorum;* Bd. V)

Bates, G.E. Byzantine coins. Cambridge, Mass.: Harvard University Press, 1971
British Museum. Dept. of Coins and Medals. Catalogue of the Imperial Byzantine coins in the British Museum 2 vols. Chicago: Argonaut, 1966 (originally published 1908)
Goodacre, H. A handbook of the coinage of the Byzantine Empire. London: Spink, 1957 (originally published 1928-33)
Hendy, M.F. Coinage and money in the Byzantine Empire, 1081-1261. Washington: Dumbarton Oaks, 1969
Whitting, P.D. Byzantine coins. New York: Putnam, 1973

Bendixen, K. Denmark's money. National Museum of Denmark, 1967

Beresford-Jones, R.D. A manual of Anglo-Gallic gold coins. London: Spink, 1964
Falkus, C. The life and times of Charles II. London: Weidenfeld and Nicolson, 1972
Farquhar, H. Portraiture of our Stuart monarchs on their coins and medals. *British Numismatic Journal* (1909) v.5
Ferguson, W.D. The coinage of Henry VII of England. *The Numismatist* (July 1947)
Grueber, H.A. Handbook of the coins of Great Britain and Ireland in the British Museum – 2nd ed. London: Spink, 1970
Henfrey, H.W. Numismata Cromwelliana: or, The medallic history of Oliver Cromwell, illustrated by his coins, medals and seals. London: J.R. Smith, 1877
Hewlett, L.M. Anglo-Gallic coins. London: Baldwin, 1920
Humphreys, H.N. The coinage of the British Empire: an outline of the progress of the coinage in Great Britain and her dependencies, from the earliest period to the present time – 3rd ed. London: Griffin, 1861
Humphreys, H.N. The gold, silver, and copper coins of England – 6th ed. London: Bonn, 1849
Linecar, H. An advanced guide to coin collecting. London: Pelham Books, 1970
Linecar, H. & A.G. Stone. English proof and pattern crown-size pieces. London: Spink, 1968
Mack, R.P. The coinage of ancient Britain. London: Spink, 1953

Select Bibliography

Austria

Byzantine Empire

Denmark

England and the United Kingdom

Nathanson, A.J. Thomas Simon; his life and work, 1618-1665. London: Seaby, 1975

North, J.J. English hammered coinage. London: Spink, 1960

Peck, C.W. English copper, tin and bronze coins in the British Museum, 1558-1958 – 2nd ed. London: Trustees of the British Museum, 1964

Rayner, P.A. The designers and engravers of the English milled coinage, 1662-1953. London: Seaby, 1954

Ridley, J. Life and times of Mary Tudor. London: Weidenfeld and Nicolson, 1974

Seaby, P.J. & P.F. Purvey. Seaby standard catalogue of British coins; vol. 1, Coins of England and the United Kingdom – 17th ed. London: Seaby, 1979

Spink and Son, Ltd. The milled coinage of England, 1662-1946 – 2nd ed. London: Spink, 1950

Vertue, G. Medals, coins, great seals, and other works of Thomas Simon – 2nd ed. London: printed by J. Nichols, 1780

Williams, N. The life and times of Elizabeth I. London: Weidenfeld and Nicolson, 1972

France   Bigot, A. Essai sur les monnaies du royaume et duche de Bretagne. Paris: Rollin, 1857

Boudeau, E. Catalogue general illustre et a prix marques de monnaies Françaises (nationales) – Nouvelle ed. Paris: Cabinet de Numismatique, N.D.

Germany   Davenport, J.S. German church and city talers, 1600-1700. Galesburg, Ill.: the author, 1967

Davenport, J.S. German talers, 1700-1800. London: Spink, 1965

Erbstein, J. & A. Erbstein. Die Ritter von Schulthess-Rechberg'sche Münz-u Medaillen-Sammlung. Lawrence, Mass.: Quarterman Publications, 1974

Hazlitt, W.C. The coinage of the European continent with catalogues of mints, denominations, and rulers. London: Swan Sonneyschein, 1893, supp. 1897

Krause, H. Numismatic dictionary; English-German, German-English. Munich: Battenberg, 1971

Mey, J. de. European crown size coins and their multiples; vol. 1, Germany 1486-1599. Amsterdam: Mevious & Hirschhorn, 1975

Greece, Ancient   Baldwin, A. Facing heads on ancient Greek coins. *American Journal of Numismatics* (1909) v.43 – reprinted by C.H. McSorley, 1968

British Museum. Dept. of Coins and Medals. A catalogue of the Greek coins – 29 vols. London: Trustees of the British Museum, 1873-1927 – reprinted, Bologna: Forni, 1963-5

British Museum. Dept. of Coins and Medals. A guide to the principal coins of the Greeks, from circa. 700 BC to AD 270; based on the work of Barclay V. Head. London: Trustees of the British Museum, 1932, reprinted 1965

Gardner, P. Archaeology and the types of Greek coins. Chicago: Argonaut, 1965 (originally published 1883)

Gardner, P. A history of ancient coinage, 700-300 BC. Oxford: Clarendon, 1918

Hammond, N.G.L. & H.H. Scullard, *eds*. Oxford classical dictionary – 2nd rev. ed. Oxford University Press, 1970

Hands, A.W. Common Greek coins. London: Spink, 1907

Head, B.V. Historia numorum; a manual of Greek numismatics – new and enl. ed. Oxford: Clarendon, 1887

Hirmer, M. Griechische Münzen Siziliens. Leipzig: Insel-Verlag, 1952

Jenkins. G.K. Coins of Greek Sicily. London: British Museum, 1966

Jenkins, G.K. & H. Kuthmann. Münzen der Griechen. Munich: Battenberg, 1972

Kraay, C.M. Greek coins. London: Thames & Hudson, 1966

Kraay, C.M. Greek coins and history; some current problems. London: Methuen, 1969

Macdonald, G. Coin types, their origin and development; being the Rhind lectures for 1904. Chicago: Argonaut, 1969 (originally published 1905)

Muller, L. The coinage of Alexander the Great; followed by a supplement containing the coins of Philip II, III and Lysimachus. New York: Attic Books, 1976 (originally published 1855, 1858)

Pozzi, S. Monnaies Grecques antiques. Zurich: Bank Leu, 1966

Robinson, E.S.G. & M.C. Hipolito. A catalogue of the Calouste Gulbenkian collection of Greek coins; part 1, Italy, Sicily, Carthage. Lisbon: Fundacao Calouste Gulbenkian, 1971

Seltman, C.T. Greek coins; a history of metallic currency and coinage down to the fall of the Hellenistic kingdoms. 2nd ed. London: Methuen, 1955

Seltman, C.T. Masterpieces of Greek coinage; essay and commentary. Oxford: Cassirer, 1949

Smith, W. Classical dictionary of biography, mythology and geography – 13th ed. London: Seaby, 1972 (originally published 1873)

Svoronos, J. & B.V. Head. The illustrations of the Historia numorum, an atlas of Greek numismatics, edited by A.M. Cresap. Chicago: Argonaut, 1968

India   Pridmore, F. The coins of the British Commonwealth of nations to the end of the reign of George VI, 1952: pt 4; India: v.1; East India Company presidency series c1642-1835. London: Spink, 1975

Japan   Jacobs, N. & Vermeule, C.C. Japanese coinage. *Includes* Catalogue of the coins of Japan, Modern Korea and Manchukuo – 2nd ed. New York: Numismatic Review, 1972

Munro, N.G. Coins of Japan. Yokohama, 1904, reprinted 1962

Numismatic Dealers Association. Encyclopaedia of Japanese coins and paper money, including Korea, Manchuria ancient gold and silver coins and modern paper money. Tokyo, 1970-1, 1973-6

Jewish   Hendin, D. Guide to ancient Jewish coins. New York: Attic Books, 1976

Kadman, L. The coins of the Jewish War of 66-73 C.E. Tel Aviv: Schocken, 1960 *(Corpus nummorum Palaestinensium*, 2nd ser.; v.3)

Kinder, A. Coins of the land of Israel; a catalogue of the collection of the Bank of Israel, Jerusalem. Jerusalem: Ketter, 1974

Meshorer, Y. Jewish coins of the Second Temple Period. Tel Aviv: Am Hassefer, 1967

Reiffenberg, A. Ancient Jewish coins – 4th ed. Jerusalem: Mass, 1965

Reifenberg, A. Israel's history in coins from the Maccabees to the Roman conquest. London: East and West Library, 1953

Romanoff, P. Jewish symbols on ancient Jewish coins. Philadelphia: Dropsie College, 1944

Netherlands and Colonies   Bucknill, J. The coins of the Dutch East Indies. London: Spink, 1931

Caerte oft lyste inhoudende den prijs (coins and mintmasters up to 1619). Antwerpen: Verdussen, 1620

Davenport, J.S. European crowns, 1600-1700. Galesburg, Ill.: the author, 1974

Delmonte, A. Le Benelux d'or; repertoire du monnayage d'or des territoires composant les anciennnes Pays-Bas. Amsterdam: Schulman, 1964

Gelder, H.E. De Nederlandse munten. Utrecht: Aula-Bocken, 1965

Scholten, C. The coins of the Dutch overseas territories, 1601-1948. Amsterdam: Schulman, 1953

Schulman, J. Handbook van de Nederlandsche munten van 1795- Amsterdam: Schulman, 1946, 1962

Zonnebloem, Uitgave van Uitgeverij. Catalogus munten van de Verenigde Oostindische Compagnie en van Nederlands Indie, 1594-1949. Amsterdam: the author, 1975

358

Batalha Reis, P. Precario das moedas Portuguesas de 1140-1940. Lisbon: 1956-8 *Portugal*

Ferraro Vaz, J. Catalogo das moedas Portuguesas . . . Portugal continental, 1640-1948. Lisbon: 1948

Ferraro Vaz, J. Livro das moedas de Portugal. Book of the coins of Portugal. Braga: 1969

Ferraro Vaz, J. Numaria medieval Portuguesa, 1128-1383. 2 vols. Lisbon: 1960

Lisbon. Casa da Moeda. Estatistica das moedas de ouro, prata, cobre e bronze que se cunharam na casa de Moeda de Lisboa; desde 1752-1871, segundo consta das respectivas libros que existem na mesma reparticao. Lisbon: Casa da Moeda, 1873

Babelon, E.C.F. Description historique et chronologique des monnaies de la Republique Romaine vulgairement appelées monnaies con- *Rome, Ancient* sulaires – 2 vols. Bologna: Forni, 1963 (originally published 1885-6)

British Museum. Dept. of Coins and Medals. Coins of the Roman Empire in the British Museum – 6 vols in 7. London: Trustees of the British Museum, 1923-62, 1965-

Cohen, H. Description historique des monnaies frappées sous l'Empire Romain communement appelées medailles imperiales – 2nd ed. 8 vols. Graz: Akademische Druck-U. Verlagstalt, 1955 (originally published 1880-92)

Hill, G.F. Historical Roman coins. Chicago: Argonaut, 1966 (originally published 1909)

Kent, J.P.C. Roman coins. London: Thames and Hudson, 1978

Mattingly, H. & E.A. Sydenham. The Roman Imperial coinage. 8 vols in 11. London: Spink, 1968

Seaby, B.A., Ltd. A catalogue of roman coins/compiled by G. Askew. London: Seaby, 1948

Sear, D.R. Roman coins and their values – 2nd rev. ed. London: Seaby, 1974

Stern, J. Historical implications of Roman coins; a survey of Roman coinage and its role in deciphering history. La Mesa, Ca.: Historia, 1975

Lhotka, J.F. & P.K. Anderson. Survey of medieval Iberian coinages. Colorado Springs: American Numismatic Assoc., 1963 (reprinted *Spain* for *The Numismatist*)

Vicenti, J.A. Catalogo general de la moneda Espanola; imperio Espanol (Europa), Fernado II Fernando I, 1475-1825. Madrid: the author, 1976

Switzerland

Divo, J-P. & Tobler E. Die Münzen der Schweiz im 19 und 20 Jahrhundert. Zurich: Hess-Leu, 1967

Lohner, C. Die Münzen der Republik Bern. Zurich: Meyer & Zeller, 1846

Mildenberg, L. Zurcher Münzen und Medaillen. Zurich: Rechberg, 1969

United States of America

Crosby, S.S. The early coins of America, and the laws governing their issue . . . Boston: the author, 1875, 1945, 1965, 1974

Durst, S.J. Comprehensive guide to American colonial coinage; its origins, history, and value. New York: the author, 1976

Newman, E.P. & Doty, R.D *eds*. Studies on money in early America. New York: American Numismatic Society, 1976

Noe, S.P. The New England and willow tree coinages of Massachussets. New York: American Numismatic Society, 1943 (*Numismatic notes and monographs*, no. 102)

Noe, S.P. The pine tree coinage of Massachusetts. New York: American Numismatic Society, 1952 (*Numismatic notes and monographs*, no. 125)

Reed, M. Encyclopedia of U.S. coins – 2nd ed. Chicago: Regnery, 1972

Scott, K. Counterfeiting in colonial America. New York: Oxford University Press, 1957

General

Angell, N. The story of money. Garden city, N.Y.: Garden City Publishing, 1929

Barber, R. A companion to world mythology. Harmondsworth: Kestrel, 1979

Becker, T.W. The coin makers. Garden City, N.Y.: Doubleday, 1969

Boutell, C. Heraldry/revised by J.P. Brooke-Little. London: Warne, 1973

Brewer, E.C, Brewer's dictionary of phrase and fable/revised by I.H. Evans – centenary ed. London: Cassell, 1970

Chamberlain, C.C. The teach yourself guide to numismatics; an A.B.C. of coins and coin collecting. London: English Universities Press, 1960

Cipolla, C., *ed*. The Middle Ages. London: Fontana, 1972. (Economic history of Europe series)

Clain-Stefanelli, E.E. The beauty and lore of coins, currency and medals. Croton-on-Hudson, N.Y.: Riverwood Pub., 1974

Clain-Stefanelli, E.E. Select numismatic bibliography. New York: Stack, 1965

Cooper, J.C. An illustrated encyclopaedia of traditional symbols. London: Thames and Hudson, 1978

Crowther, G. An outline of money – 2nd rev. ed. London: Nelson, 1948

Frey, A.R. Dictionary of numismatic names: with Glossary of numismatic terms in English, French, German, Italian, Swedish, by M.M. Salton. London: Spink, 1973 (originally published 1917)

Grun, B. The timetables of history; a chronology of world events. London: Thames and Hudson, 1975

Hall, E.T. & D.M. Metcalf, *eds.* Methods of chemical and metallurgical investigation of ancient coinage; a symposium held by the Royal Numismatic Society, London, 1970. London: Royal Numismatic Society, 1972 (*Royal Numismatic Society. Special publication;* no. 8)

Hobson, B. & R. Obojski. Illustrated encyclopedia of world coins. Garden City, N. Y.: Doubleday, 1970

Jung, C.G. Man and his symbols. London: Aldus, 1964

Karlson, G. Library catalogue of the American Numismatic Association – 2nd ed. Colorado Springs: American Numismatic Assoc., 1977

Milne, J.G., G.H.V. Sutherland & J.D.A. Thompson. Coin collecting. London: Oxford University Press, 1950

Porteous, J. Coins in history; a survey of coinage from the reform of Diocletian to the Latin Monetary Union. New York: Putnam, 1969

Price, M.J. & B.L. Trell. Coins and their cities; architecture on the ancient coins of Greece, Rome and Palestine. London: Vecchi, 1977

Rawlings, G.B. Coins and how to know them. Chicago: Ammon Press, 1966 (originally published 1908)

Reader's Digest. History of man; the last two million years. London: Readers Digest, 1974

Reinfeld, F. Treasury of world's coins/revised by B. Hobson. New York: Sterling, 1967

Hill, G.F. Becker, the counterfeiter. London: Spink, 1955 (originally published 1925)

Newman, E.P. Lessons in modern day counterfeiting. *From* 'Coin forgery approaches perfection'. Copenhagen: International Numismatic Congress, 1967. *The Numismatist* (Nov. 1967)

Counterfeiting

Adams, Ansell. Artificial light photography. Dobbs Ferry, N.Y.: Morgan, 1968

Adams, Ansell. Natural light photography. Dobbs Ferry, N.Y.: Morgan, 1969

Applied infra-red photography. Rochester, N.Y.: Kodak, 1980 (Series M-28)

Basic developing, printing, enlarging in black-and-white. Rochester, N.Y.: Kodak, 1979 (Series AJ-2)

Photography

Photography continued

Close-up photography and photomacrography. Rochester, N.Y.: Kodak, 1977 (Series N-12)

Eaton, G.T. Photographic chemistry in black-and-white and colour – 2nd ed. Hastings-on-Hudson, N.Y.: Morgan, 1965

Electron microscopy and photography. Rochester, N.Y.: Kodak, 1973 (Series P-236)

Giebelhausen, J., *ed.* Manual of applied photography. London: Fountain, 1966

Giebelhausen, J. Photography in industry. Munich: Grossbild-Technik, 1967

Neblette, C.B. & A.E. Murray. Photographic lenses. Dobbs Ferry, N.Y.: Morgan, 1973

Photolab design. Rochester, N.Y.: Kodak, 1978 (Series K-13)

Practical densitometry. Rochester, N.Y.: Kodak, 1979 (Series E-59)

Printing color negatives. Rochester, N.Y.: Kodak, 1978 (Series E-66)

Thomas, D.B. Cameras, photographs and accessories. London: HMSO, 1966 (Science Museum illustrated booklet)

Ultra-violet and fluorescence photography. Rochester, N.Y., Kodak, 1974 (Series M-27)

Understanding graininess and granularity. Rochester, N.Y.: Kodak, 1979 (Series F-20)

What is B/W quality . . . and how to get it? Rochester, N.Y.: Kodak, 1979 (Series G-4)

Why a color may not reproduce correctly. Rochester, N.Y.: Kodak, 1978 (Series E-73)

Zakia, R.D. & H.N. Todd. Color primer I & II. Dobbs Ferry, N.Y.: Morgan, 1974

The marks caused by the removal of small scrapings of metal to adjust overweight coins.

Adjustment marks

Two objects or creatures back to back.

Addorsed

An impenetrable defence, shield of Zeus, Athene and Apollo, usually represented as a snake, gorgon, or a short goatskin cloak worn over the left arm.

Aegis

A vessel for sacred use.

Ampulla

A hairband (or part thereof) above the forehead.

Ampyx

An object worn as a charm against evil.

Amulet

A small ring (archit.); small fillet encircling a column.

Annulet

A fifteenth century helmet consisting of a globular iron cap spreading out into a projection over the back of the neck and in front, a visor.

Armet

Masonry constructed of square hewn stones.

Ashlars

An extinct species of European Wild Ox.

Aurochs

A double watch-tower erected over a gate or bridge as an outer defence to a city or castle.

Barbican

A field divided horizontally into equal parts by bars of alternating tincture.

Barry

A steel helmet with a pointed dome, often with a visor, and a camail to protect the neck and shoulders.

Basinet

Benedictine	The religious order of monks founded by St. Benedict, circa 529 AD.
Biga	A chariot drawn by two horses.
Blank	Synonymous with plachet, a prepared metal disc on which coins are impressed.
Broad	English hammered gold coin of twenty shillings first issued in 1604. The term was applied after the introduction of the Guinea in 1663 to differentiate the (broader) Unite from the new milled coins.
Bullion	Bullion in the numismatic context usually refers to unwrought gold or silver as distinguished from coin or manufactured articles.
Byzantine	Of Byzantium or Constantinople, Eastern Roman Empire (395 – 1453 AD).
Calligraphy	Beautiful writing.
Caparison	Cloth cape, armour or other covering, usually gaily ornamented, spread over the saddle or harness of a horse or other beast of burden.
Cartouche	An ornamental scroll and/or oval containing a device or inscription.
Chequey	A chequered field.
Chiton	A tunic or frock of ancient Greece.
Cinquefoil	Ornamental floral form of five leaves; ornament of five cusps within a circle or square.

The portrait, figure, object, symbol, inscription or other distinguishing device on a coin. — *Coin type*

Dies damaged by violent, direct contact with each other. — *Clashed dies*

A single row of chequers. — *Compony*

In heraldry a term of blazon describing the attitude of an animal — legs and belly resting on the ground, looking forward, head erect, tail between its hind legs and the tuft of its tail erect. — *Couchant*

A fraudulent imitation of coins, banknotes, stamps, stocks, etc. — *Counterfeit*

Applied to animals represented as running. — *Courant*

Armour to protect the elbows. — *Couteres*

Small ornamental buds, curled leaves, animals and other embellishments on the inclined sides of pinnacles, gables, canopies, pediments, choir stalls, etc., in gothic architecture. — *Crockets*

A cross botonné or treflé has limbs of equal length each terminating in an ornamental trefoil. — *Cross botonné*

A cross patée or formée has triangular limbs conjoined at their apexes. — *Cross patée*

A small transverse guard on the hilt of a sword. — *Cross-piece*

A cross potent has limbs of equal size with crutch-shaped ends. — *Cross potent*

Armour; the breast plate and back plate fastened together, originally leather and later steel. — *Cuirass*

Cunieform	Ancient inscriptions composed of wedge-shaped or arrow-headed elements.
Cusp	The projecting point formed by contiguous arches.
Debasement	Reduction in the purity (fineness) and thus the value of a coin or currency, by alloying, reducing the weight, or in the case of paper currency, reducing the gold reserves (backing).
Deified	Considered or treated as a god.
Denticles	Small toothlike patterns or projections.
Diadem	A fillet worn by the kings of Persia, adopted by Alexander the Great and his successors as a symbol of royal honour and dignity, often portrayed as a wreath of leaves or flowers, a crown or a headband.
Diapered	A uniform diamond-shaped reticulation used to diversify and adorn.
Die axis ↑	The die axis of a coin is usually indicated by one or two arrows, indicating the position of the reverse design relative to that of the obverse. The obverse position is always indicated or assumed to be upright.
Dipped coins	Coins of base metal coated with gold or silver as a method of counterfeiting.
Electrotype	A copy of a coin medal, etc., formed by the deposition of copper on a mould by electrolytic galvanic action.
Engrailed	A margin or edge of a coin, formed by a circle, or with a ring of pellets having a series of curvilinear indentations.

A term used to describe a charge surrounded by the rays of a sun. *En soleil*

A shield bearing a coat of arms. *Escutcheon*

A small space below the principal device of a coin, usually on the reverse, bearing the date, engraver's initials, mintmark, etc., often demarcated by a ground line. *Exergue*

False lozenge; a voided diamond-shaped figure. *Faux lozenge*

Two horizontal lines containing the central part of a shield usually occupying a third of the escutcheon. *Fess/Fesse*

Inconvertible paper currency made legal tender by decree (fiat) having insufficient reserves of noble metal or coin (backing) to support its intrinsic or promissory values. *Fiat money*

A clasp, brooch or buckle. *Fibula*

In heraldry a narrow border, band, fringing or edge of a different tincture or pattern from the rest of the charge. *Fimbriated*

The comparative purity of the coin's fabric, i.e. its freedom from alloy. *Fineness*

see planchet. *Flan*

A small ornamental flower. *Fleuret*

Perhaps best known as the heraldic lily of France. It is also used merely as an embellishment and has ancient numismatic origins. *Fleur-de-lis*

A flower shaped ornament on coins, architecture, etc. *Fleuron*

Fleury	Decorated with fleurs-de-lis especially a cross with its limbs so tipped.
Floriated	Embellished with floral ornaments.
Folliaged	Decorated with a representation of foliage.
Follis (Latin)	Leather money bag; later a term applied to a copper coin in the time of Diocletian's reform, circa 296 AD.
Fuller	The blood channel — a fluted groove on the blade of a sword.
Gauntlet	A glove worn as part of a suit of armour usually made of leather covered with steel plates.
Globus Cruciger	*see* orb.
Gorget	Armour for the throat.
Gyronny	A field divided into triangular sections (gyrons) radiating from the middle (fess point).
Hide of Land	Defined in Anglo-Saxon times as the area that could be ploughed in one year with a single plough; the amount adequate to support one family and its dependants.
Himation	An oblong drape originally worn by the ancient Greeks as an outer garment.
Inescutcheon	A small escutcheon, charged on a larger escutcheon.
Ingot	A metal casting or billet usually in the form of an oblong brick with convergent sides; used as a convenient device for storing and/or transporting gold, silver, iron, etc.

A term referring to the mintmark when it is positioned at the beginning of the legend of a coin.   *Initial mark*

The lower or interior curve of an arch.   *Intrados*

A form of line pattern comprised of outward convex curves.   *Invected*

Rising up or emerging from a chief.   *Issuant*

Lewd; pertaining to the phallus carried at Bacchic festivals.   *Ithyphallic*

A close fitting tunic or doublet worn by knights, fashionable in the fourteenth century, usually made of leather, but sometimes of padded material. Later a surcoat of richly emblazoned sleeveless material worn over armour.   *Jupon*

A scarf or mantling worn over the helmet as a covering for protection from the elements; or as a decorative accessory.   *Lambrequin*

A Latin cross has a longer lower line than the others.   *Latin cross*

An illuminator of manuscripts and/or painter of portraits.   *Limner*

Armour composed of metal rings or plates.   *Mail, Coat of*

The science and system of weights and measures.   *Metrology*

Coins struck by machine, so named from the water mills or horse drawn mills which powered the minting machinery, or coins with fluted or grooved edges.   *Milled coins*

Mark included in the design of the coin to indicate the mint, moneyer or date. *See also* initial mark, privy mark.   *Mintmark*

A tall cap, deeply cleft at the top, worn by Bishops and   *Mitre*

Abbots as a symbol of office.

Nimbus A halo.

Numismatic Pertaining to the archaeology, history, metrology and artistic study of coins and medals.

Numismatist One who has a special interest in numismatics, a collector and/or student of coins.

Ogee A pair of S-shaped curves used in profile to form a pointed arch.

Overstriking A coin struck on a previously minted planchet instead of a newly prepared one.

Palewise Party per pale. The heraldic term to describe a shield divided vertically into two equal parts of different tinctures.

Panache A tuft or plume of feathers, forming the crest on a helmet.

Panoply A complete suit of armour.

Parapet A low defensive wall at the edge of a rampart, balcony, roof, etc.

Passant guardant The heraldic term to describe the attitude of a beast walking – head facing the spectator, three paws on the ground, the right forepaw raised and tail curved over the back.

Patina The natural alteration of the surface of a coin produced by a film or incrustation formed over a period of time through oxidation and other environmental influences often enriching the specimen. (Hence patinated or toned.)

A piece minted for a proposed issue, submitted for consideration by the issuing authority. *Pattern*

Armour to protect the shoulders; armoured shoulder plates. *Pauldrons*

In heraldry a charge representing a broad barbed arrow, sometimes with an engrailed inner edge. *Pheon*

A small ornamental turret or spire. *Pinnacle*

Blank metal disc of correct weight and fineness used for the striking of coin; also referred to as a flan or a blank. *Planchet*

The lower member of a column, pedestal or block serving as a base to a statue, bust, furniture, ornament, etc. *Plinth*

A knob, round boss or spherical ornament terminating the hilt of a sword; also used generally as an embellishment. *Pommel*

A covered approach to the entrance of a building. *Porch*

A fortified gateway comprised of vertical and horizontal iron bars, the former being barbed at the lower end. *Portcullis*

A member of the bodyguard of a Roman military commander or Emperor. *Praetorian prefect*

A secret mark incorporated in the design of a coin as a means of identification of the moneyer. Privy marks took the form of a peculiar punctuation mark, a deliberate spelling error, the inclusion of a device between the inscription, or a misshapen letter, etc. *Privy Mark*

A chariot drawn by four horses (or elephants) harnessed abreast. *Quadriga*

Quatrefoil	Ornament or tracery of four cusps usually representing a leaf or a flower.
Rampant	A term to describe the attitude of a beast portrayed in heraldry — standing erect, one hind paw on the ground, the other three raised, looking forward with its tail erect.
Rampart	A walkway on top of a defensive wall for troops, guns, etc., usually surmounted by stone parapets.
Remedy	The tolerance allowed in the purity and weight of a coin.
Repoussé	Ornamental metal-work raised in relief by hammering from the reverse side.
Roundel	A circular ornament, clasp, brooch, medallion, etc.
Sabatons	Armed shoes worn by knights and warriors, probably from the thirteenth century, composed of steel plates or scales, with broad rounded or square toes.
Saltire	A diagonal cross.
Satyr	A composite woodland god or demon, partly man, partly horse.
Semé-de-lis	Strewn with fleurs-de-lis.
Serpentine	A dull green rock or mineral with markings resembling those of a serpent's skin, chiefly of hydrous magnesium silicate. It was used in antiquity for seals, jewellery and ornaments.
Soleil, En	*see* En Soleil.
Sollerets	Armed shoes worn by knights and warriors in the fourteenth

and fifteenth centuries, composed of steel plates or scales with pointed toes.

The spaces between the shoulders of contiguous arches and their surrounding border often filled with embellishment. *Spandrels*

Coins of noble metal as opposed to coins of little intrinsic worth used as mere tokens. *Specie*

The art of using a spectrograph, an instrument used for photographing the spectrum. *Spectrography*

The art of using a spectrometer, an instrument for measuring the index of refraction. *Spectrometry*

A fillet or headband with a sling-shaped hairnet, worn by women in ancient Greece. *Sphendone*

A small wheel with sharp radial points forming part of a spur. *Spur Rowel*

A short vividly emblazoned surcoat worn by kings, heralds and knights, or a coarse garment worn by the lower classes. *Tabard*

see patina. *Toned*

Delicate lines or decoratively shaped openings, networks, interlacings, etc., as found in architecture; incorporated as an ornamental element in certain coin designs. *Tracery*

An ornamental figure representing a trifoliate leaf. *Trefoil*

A numismatic term borrowed from heraldry describing a series of arches or other design containing the type or distinctive device of a coin. *Tressure*

Trident   A three-pronged weapon, fish spear or sceptre; an attribute of the sea god Poseidon or Neptune and borne by Britannia.

Turrets   Small towers often set upon castles as a defence.

Tutenag   A white alloy of zinc, copper, and nickel with a small quantity of iron, silver or arsenic, said to have been originally imported from China and the East Indies.

Unite   A gold coin of England originally issued by James I in 1604, current at twenty shillings (raised in 1611 to twenty-two shillings). The Unite was so called as an indirect reference to the union of the crowns under King James.

Vambraces   Armour for the forearms.

Vair   Fur from a squirrel with a grey back and a white belly used as trimming or lining for garments especially in the thirteenth and fourteenth centuries. One of the furs of heraldry usually represented as azure (blue) and argent (white) tinctured bell or cup-shaped pieces disposed alternately.

Watermarks   A subtle distinctive mark or device usually impressed into quality paper during manufacture, generally only visible when held against the light.

The Arms of the Duchy of Brunswick – Wolfenbüttel are adorned with floral ornature and surmounted by five crested helmets heightened with coronets. The central crest of the Dukes of Brunswick and Lüneburg consists of a column, surmounted by a crown, between two facing sickles embellished with peacock rosettes. In front of the column is a horse courant left (the heraldic ensign of Brunswick and Hanover). To the right of the principal crest is the helmet of the Counts of Bruchhausen which carries eight vertical lances with pennants, flanked by the horns of an aurochs. The helmet on the extreme right bears attires (antlers of a stag) from the crests of Regenstein and Blankenburg and a pair of aurochs horns, the crest of Diepholz. The extreme left hand crest has a panache of peacock's feathers, the crest of Lauterberg, which is flanked by attires – the crest of the Counts of Honstein.

The Arms of Brunswick-Wolfenbüttel

The escutcheon bore quarterly:

1. Semé of hearts and a lion rampant – *Lüneburg*. 2. Two lions passant guardant in pale – *Brunswick*. 3. A lion rampant, crowned – *Everstein*. 4. A lion rampant within a bordure compony – *Homburg*. 5. A lion rampant, crowned – from the Arms of *Diepholz*. 6. A lion rampant – the chief of the Arms of *Lauterberg*. 7. Gyronny of eight – *Bruchhausen*; two bears paws addorsed, issuant on a chief – *Hoya*. 8. An eagle elevated and displayed from the Arms of *Diepholz*. 9. Barry of six – from the Arms of *Lauterberg* and a chief chequey – *Honstein*. 10. A stag courant – *Klettenberg*. 11. Attires from the Arms of *Regenstein* and *Blankenburg*.

ABC Press (Pty) Ltd, Cape Town – Steve Avery, Roger Bolton, Klaus Borgelt,
Roy Christian, Vida Fisher, Robin Frandsen Alan Hambidge, Tom Scully,
Gordon Wanstall
American Numismatic Association, Colorado – Ed Fleischmann, Geneva Karlson
American Numismatic Society, New York – Michael Di Biasy
The Archives, Cape Town
Armstrong and Botha, Cape Town – Cyril Alban Armstrong
Ashmolean Museum, Oxford – Dr D.M. Metcalf
A.H. Baldwin & Sons Ltd, London – Edward Baldwin
The Bible Society of South Africa, Cape Town – Julia Smuts
Studio Briggs Ltd, London – Ted Harrison
The British Museum, London – J. Cribb, Dr G.K. Jenkins
Bank Leu A G, Zürich – Silvia Hurter
City Coins, Cape Town – Natalie Jaffe
Danish National Museum, Copenhagen – Kirsten Bendixen
Peter Davey, London
Design – Gerhard Schwekendiek
J.A. Duggan & Co. Ltd, Blackburn – John Duggan
Editor – Nicola Helen Legg, Constantia
Final Editor – Gillian Loubser, Constantia
Fitzwilliam Museum, Cambridge – Janine Bourriau, Terence Volk
J. Paul Getty Museum, Malibu – J. Frel, John Twilley
German Heraldic Association, Wiesbaden – Dr. Ottfried Neubecker
German Numismatic Society
Trevor Hayward, Cape Town
Hirt & Carter (Pty) Ltd, Cape Town – Malcolm Smith, Nigel Webb,
   Martin West, Bruce Mackenzie
Index – Ethleen Lastovica
International Bureau for the Suppression of Counterfeit Coins,
   London – E.G.V. Newman
Roy Johannesson, Cape Town
Kodak (South Africa) Ltd, Cape Town – Peggy Coetzer, Basil Karlse, Peter Moore
Line Illustration – Tobie Beele
The Metropolitan Police Forensic Science Laboratory, London
The Trustees of the National Gallery, London
Royal Mint, London – Grahame Dyer
Prisman and Wilson, Cape Town – Cyril Prisman
B.A. Seaby Ltd, London – Margaret Amstel, Frank Purvey, Peter Seaby
Jean Small, Constantia
Smithsonian Institution, Washington – Vladimir Clain-Stefanelli

Acknowledgements

South African Cultural History Museum, Cape Town – Lalou Meltzer,
    Dr W. Schneewind
South African Library, Cape Town
South African Numismatic Society, Cape Town – Walter Bergman, J.W. Brett,
    Dr B. Chavda, Helmut Cohn, Carl Ernst Heinrich, Bill Hibbard, Robert James,
    Richard Mann, Dr Frank Mitchell
Spink & Son Ltd, London – Douglas Liddell, Howard Linecar, George Muller,
    Douglas Saville
Spink & Son Numismatics, Zürich – Dr Jean-Paul Divo
Swedish State Museum – Dr Ulla Westemark
Frank R. Thorold Ltd – Robin Fryde
University of Cape Town: Department of Classics – Dr J.E. Atkinson;
    Department of German – Gisela Pardoe;
    Department of Hebrew Studies – Professor S. Hopkins;
    The Jagger Library;
    Leslie Library – Sarah Diamant
Peter Woodhead, London.

Index

380

To Mr. Addison,

Occassioned by his Dialogues on MEDALS *

Alexander Pope (1688 – 1744)

See the wild Waste of all-devouring years!
How Rome her own sad Sepulchre appears,
With nodding arches, broken temples spread!
The very Tombs now vanish'd like their dead!
Imperial wonders rais'd on Nations spoil'd,
Where mix'd with Slaves the groaning Martyr toil'd;
Huge Theatres, that now unpeopled Woods,
Now drain'd a distant country of her Floods;
Fanes, which admiring Gods with pride survey,
Statues of Men, scarce less alive than they;
Some felt the silent stroke of mould'ring age,
Some hostile fury, some religious rage;
Barbarian blindness, Christian zeal conspire,
And Papal piety, and Gothic fire.
Perhaps, by its own ruins sav'd from flame,
Some bury'd marble half preserves a name;
That Name the learn'd with fierce disputes pursue,
And give to Titus old Vespasian's due.
 Ambition sigh'd; She found it vain to trust
the faithless Column and the crumbling Bust;
Huge moles, whose shadow stretch'd from shore to shore,
Their ruins ruin'd, and their place no more!
Convinc'd, she now contracts her vast design,
And all her Triumphs shrink into a Coin:
A narrow orb each crouded conquest keeps,
Beneath her Palm here sad Judaea weeps,
Here scantier limits the proud Arch confine,
And scarce are seen the prostrate Nile or Rhine,
A small Euphrates thro' the piece is roll'd,
And little Eagles wave their wings in gold.
 The Medal, faithful to its charge of fame,
Thro' climes and ages bears each form and name:
In one short view subjected to your eye

Gods, Emp'rors, Heroes, Sages, Beauties, lie.
With sharpen'd sight pale Antiquaries pore,
Th' inscription value, but the rust adore;
This the blue varnish, that the green endears,
The sacred rust of twice ten hundred years!
To gain Pescennius one employs his schemes,
One grasps a Cecrops in ecstatic dreams;
Poor Vadius, long with learned spleen devour'd,
Can taste no pleasure since his Shield was scour'd;
And Curio, restless by the Fair-one's side,
Sighs for an Otho, and neglects his bride.
 Theirs is the Vanity, the Learning thine:
Touch'd by thy hand, again Rome's glories shine,
Her Gods, and god-like Heroes rise to view,
And all her faded garlands bloom a-new.
Nor blush, these studies thy regard engage;
These pleas'd the Fathers of poetic rage;
The verse and sculpture bore an equal part,
And Art reflected images to Art.
 Oh when shall Britain, conscious of her claim,
Stand emulous of Greek and Roman fame?
In living medals see her wars enroll'd,
And vanquish'd realms supply recording gold?
Here, rising bold, the Patriot's honest face;
There Warriors frowning in historic brass:
Then future ages with delight shall see
How Plato's, Bacon's, Newton's looks agree;
Or in fair series laurell'd Bards be shown,
A Virgil there, and here an Addison.
Then shall thy CRAGS (and let me call him mine)
On the cast ore, another Pollio, shine;
With aspect open, shall erect his head,
And round the orb in lasting notes be read,
"Statesman, yet friend to Truth! of soul sincere,
"In action faithful, and in honour clear;
"Who broke no promise, serv'd no private end,
"Who gain'd no title, and who lost no friend,
"Ennobled by himself, by all approv'd,
"And prais'd, unenvy'd, by the Muse he lov'd."

*The use of the word Medal was in former time extended to
 include coins, especially numismatic specimens of artistic
 merit and historical interest.